Martha Frances

P9-DEN-190

Organic God

Martha,

May God bless you.

The Mower.

COWLEY PUBLICATIONS is a ministry of the brothers of the Society of Saint John the Evangelist, a monastic order in the Episcopal Church. Our mission is to provide books and resources for those seeking spiritual and theological formation. COWLEY PUBLICATIONS is committed to developing a new generation of writers and teachers who will encourage people to think and pray in new ways about spirituality, reconciliation, and the future.

# Organic God

 Lenten Meditations
on the Words of Jesus

*Kate Moorehead*

Cowley Publications
*Lanham, Chicago, New York, Toronto, and Plymouth, UK*

Published in the United States of America by Cowley Publications, a division of
the Society of Saint John the Evangelist. No portion of this book may be repro-
duced, stored in or introduced into a retrieval system, or transmitted, in any form
or by any means—including photocopying—without the prior written permission
of Cowley Publications, except in the case of brief quotations embedded in critical
articles and reviews.

Library of Congress Cataloging-in-Publication Data

Moorehead, Kate, 1970–
    Organic God : lenten meditations on the words of Jesus / Kate Moorehead.
        p.    cm.
    ISBN-13: 978-1-56101-283-1    ISBN-10: 1-56101-283-1    (pbk. : alk. paper)
    1. Lent—Meditations. 2. Jesus Christ—Words—Meditations. I. Title.

BV85.M59    2006
242'.34—dc22

                                                            2006024915

Scripture quotations are taken from the New Revised Standard Version of the
Bible, © 1989, by the Division of Christian Education of the National Council of
the Churches of Christ in the United States of America. Used by permission.

Cover design: Gary Ragaglia
Interior design: Wendy Holdman

This book was printed in the United States of America on acid-free paper.

A Cowley Publications Book
Published by Rowman & Littlefield Publishers, Inc.
A wholly owned subsidiary of
The Rowman & Littlefield Publishing Group, Inc.
4501 Forbes Boulevard, Suite 200, Lanham, Maryland 20706
http://www.rowmanlittlefield.com

10 Thornbury Road, Plymouth PL6 7PP, United Kingdom

Distributed by National Book Network

For the men in my life: JD, Luke, Jake, and Max

# Contents

# Preface

Jesus left his life behind and walked into the desert alone. There, for forty days and forty nights, he spent time with God. For centuries Christians have celebrated Jesus' radical discipline by following him into a spiritual desert. Long ago a season was set aside to commemorate his solitude and bravery. For forty days and forty nights, we are invited to deepen our relationship with God, to discipline ourselves in new ways, to withhold pleasure, to take on projects—anything that solidifies our commitment to the One who created us, anything that helps us listen to what God is trying to tell us. This is what God asks of us during the season that we call Lent.

Most of us cannot leave our lives behind. We are not able to walk away from everything that we know and spend forty days alone, but we can adopt a spiritual discipline. We can offer God a small portion of our day, time in which we attempt to listen more closely to the words of Jesus of Nazareth.

This book is one way to enter the season of Lent. It contains forty meditations, each of which focuses on a single image that Jesus used, a metaphor from nature. These meditations are intended to take you deep into Jesus' words, into the many dimensions of meaning contained in the simplest of his images.

These are metaphors that many of you have heard before. They are repeated often in the Christian tradition, yet rarely examined with the intensity that they deserve. Jesus offered great wisdom to us when he gave us these words. With the simplest of images, Christ can take you into profound contemplation of God. Come with me. Together let us scratch the surface of their meaning and glimpse the incredible richness contained within.

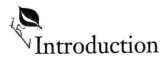

# Introduction

> *Nature is only the image, the symbol; but it is the symbol Scripture invites me to use. We are summoned to pass in through Nature, beyond her, into that splendour which she fitfully reflects.*
>
> C. S. LEWIS, *THE WEIGHT OF GLORY*, 44

Mysticism is on the rise. I see evidence of it almost every day in my parish. People are hungry for more than knowledge or wisdom: we want a personal experience of God.

Why are my parishioners so hungry for a taste of God's presence? To a certain degree, we humans have always longed for the presence of God to be made known to us, but throughout the centuries, we have often been satisfied to read about God, to study, to serve God in others. Experiential worship without grounded theology is becoming the norm in many American churches today. We clergy are racing to provide people with a genuine experience of God. The content of what we tell them seems to be secondary to the experience. People want to be touched. They want to be moved. And they want God *now*.

"Why haven't I heard God's voice yet?" one man in my parish asked. "I have been asking, I have been praying. . . . Why is God not present to me?" We are all hungry for a genuine experience of God, and yet we don't know how to wait. It is our nature to expect fast production, so why wouldn't we expect mysticism-on-tap? Why wouldn't God be prompt in responding to our needs?

I am regularly asked questions about "the spiritual life." By this term, people are often trying to allude to many aspects of themselves: their psychological health, their physical awareness, and the possibility of experiencing the divine. Because the spiritual life is so underarticulated, we have no better term to use, and no possibility of identifying its many components. Suffice it to say that the spiritual life includes the whole person and the possibility of that person experiencing God.

We join a church and, after just a month or so of attending worship, we want results. Within weeks we wonder why we haven't had a life-changing experience of the presence of God. But the spiritual life is not a computer program. We cannot approach the spiritual life as a consumer. We cannot show up at the church, expect McEucharist, and sense the divine all before lunch. An experience of the presence of God cannot be controlled in such a manner. It is this fact that frustrates and even stalls the faith development of many of us.

We need new insight to convey the mystery of the spiritual

in this age of information. To discover the organic nature of God's interaction with us, we have only to look to Jesus.

I was just four years old when the man next door invited me to his backyard. "I am a gardener," he said. "Would you like to plant some flowers with me?"

My memories are distant. I recall digging in rich dirt, black mounds molding to my little fingers, worms sliding into view, bulbs with their crusty surfaces. And Maynard Mack, puttering beside me, planting flowers.

He was a professor of Shakespeare at Yale, but I could not conceive of this at the time, nor did I care. All I knew was his warm garden, full to bursting with color and movement. All I knew was that I loved to plant.

For thousands of years, human beings have lived intimately with Mother Earth. We have worked her soil, watched her moods swing with the seasons, ached with her droughts. The life of a farmer was a life of relationship: with the soil, the wind, the sun and the moon. The intricacies of this relationship became our survival guide. We lived by listening to the earth.

Today most of us no longer live by listening to the earth; we listen instead to the satisfying ring of the cash register. Our rap technological development has resulted in our estranger from matter itself. Instead of feeling the dirt mold betw fingers, we spend more time indoors. We do not sniff the air to determine the weather, we flip on the television. And whereas determining the weather once determined our productivity and made our survival dependent on the moods of the earth, today it is more often a matter of determining whether we need to bring an umbrella to work. The organic pace of the seasons is becoming lost to us. We buy grapefruit in November and bananas in March. We have divorced ourselves from our source. We are forgetting how to love the earth.

Estrangement from our planet is a spiritual issue. As we remove ourselves from the natural rhythm of organic life, we lose an important dimension of the life of the spirit. For the life of devotion to God closely resembles the life of nature. As we forget the rhythms of our planet, the spiritual life itself also becomes harder to comprehend. As we lose touch with an aspect of the creation, we also lose touch with our intuitive sense of God's presence.

Jesus possessed a deep connection to the earth, a connection that he referred to often in his ministry. The more we remove ourselves from the earth, the more it becomes difficult to understand his message.

Throughout his ministry Jesus of Nazareth taught using parables of planting. Over and over again, he likened the journey toward God to the movement of nature. Earth and its seasons, planting and watering—this was the language of Galilee at the time of the Gospel writers. God chose to become incarnate in a land of farmers and fishermen, in a time when people lived off the land without refrigeration. When Jesus spoke of trees, of seeds and soil, he was speaking a language of deep meaning. Everyone around him knew the feel of soil between their fingers, knew the toil and necessity of planting and watering. True to his incarnational purpose, Jesus was expressing the language of God through the language of those around him, the language of organic life.

In my years as a priest, I have found no better analogy for the spiritual life than that of a growing plant. The spiritual life cannot be approached as we would tackle a computer program or a technological glitch. The spiritual life must be gradually nurtured as we would a plant. Once we understand our relationship with God as something organic, as a plant, then we understand that just as a plant needs to be regularly watered and nourished and given sunlight, so we need to relate with God on a regular basis. Just as a plant does not thrive if it is overwatered, so I would not expect a new believer to attend an eight-day silent retreat, having never established a disciplined life of prayer—and risk drowning her or his newly found faith.

So, to uncover the great mysteries of these rich parables, we return to the earth. Take off your gloves, your shoes, and your socks. Let your toes sink into the rich soil. Grab handfuls of life's abundance. Breathe the air and watch the wind rustle the leaves in the trees. As the winter evaporates into spring and the world around you blooms to full flower, consider that reminders of God lie all around you: in the seeds, in the trees and flowers. God's life is ever present to us in nature. Once we stop and look, we realize that God is communicating with us all the time. The secrets of God's life with us are revealed to us every day in nature itself. We are surrounded by icons of God's presence, parables of planting.

During this season of Lent, take a few moments each day to ponder the richness of these metaphors. Plumb their depths, explore the tiniest of details, live along with the beauty and the terror of organic life. Discover how much Jesus gave to us when he compared the spiritual life to nature.

In this book I have devoted each of the seven weeks of Lent to a theme that Jesus addressed frequently. On each day of the week, we will explore an aspect of this particular theme or metaphor, finding meaning within the smallest details. Gaze with me upon these icons of the spiritual life. As you return with me to nature, I pray that you will find yourself living more intimately with God.

# CHAPTER 1

# The Lilies of the Field

*Ash Wednesday–Saturday*

# Ash Wednesday

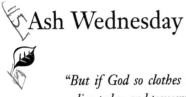

A woman in my church lost twin girls at birth. The doctors could not revive them. By the time I arrived at the hospital, they were both dead. Their mother looked up at me. Her voice was hoarse from the pain. "Are they all right?" she asked me through her weeping. This was a moment beyond theology, beyond rational explanation. I didn't think. I just blurted out, "I believe that God will take care of them."

I looked out the hospital window and the wind blew the leaves of a tree. I felt that God was there. And I believed that, even though their hearts had stopped beating, they were alive in God. We prayed over those tiny bodies. To this day I believe that God cares for them somewhere far beyond our understanding. But I nonetheless don't understand why God did not allow them to stay with their mother.

How can we believe that God will take care of us when people die of starvation all over the world? What does it mean that God cares for the grass of the field when sometimes it is trampled beneath our feet? Could it be that there is more to life than physical comfort, even than survival? What if there is another, deeper world that we cannot see? What if God holds our souls in life, as the psalmist writes, even when our bodies fail?

Jesus tells us that he cares for the grass. He tells us that God is actually looking out for plant life, watching over the smallest of creatures. God even watches out for those insignificant pieces of grass that no one notices, that live for one season only and then return to the earth.

What did Jesus mean when he said that God will take care of us as God takes care of the grass? I can only hope that Jesus was telling us what we long to hear—that there is more to life than the limitations of a physical body, that our souls are held in life, that they are more beautiful than the most elegant flower, and that God will care for them. It is my belief that God will preserve our essence into another existence, an existence more significant, more profound, more timeless than the one in which we live. In the fullness of time, God will never let us go.

After praying over the bodies of those twin babies, I drove home in the wee hours of the morning, conscious of my own breath and thankful to be alive. Life is so incredible, so fragile, so beautiful, so precarious.

# First Thursday in Lent

> *"And can any of you by worrying add a single hour to your span of life? If then you are not able to do so small a thing as that, why do you worry about the rest? Consider the lilies, how they grow: they neither toil nor spin; yet I tell you, even Solomon in all his glory was not clothed like one of these."*

LUKE 12:25–27

## The Soaring of the Soul

Jonathan came to my office for advice. He had been junior warden of the church, had a flourishing career, was an accomplished pianist—and then he suffered a stroke. He awoke with a different body and mind. His thoughts were all jumbled. He couldn't speak. He found it nearly impossible to put one foot in front of the other and, worst of all, he couldn't play the piano.

With his wife by his side, Jonathan began the long journey of rehabilitation. Three years later he could speak simple sentences, but he still frequently lost his train of thought. He sat in my office with tears in his eyes, unable to articulate his grief. His wife interpreted his tears for me. She described how often he cried, that he would sit in front of the piano at home weeping. He cried because his music was inside him but he could no longer express it.

"I used to go there," he said. "I used to play there and it came out. . . . It just came . . . my feelings, my everything. And now . . . it can't come out."

Jonathan could no longer make the sign of the cross in church. He could not kneel at the altar rail. He dropped the communion wafer. When he tried to read the Bible at night, his mind skipped around. He could not focus his eyes. And he could not even adequately express his frustration.

"I cannot pray!" he told me. "I cannot read! I cannot bow! I cannot kneel!"

We sat together as he cried. After the tears, calm came. It was clear to me that in fact he was praying better than ever before. For though Jonathan's body had been crippled, his heart and soul had soared to new heights. His love of God was so great and so intense as to be overwhelming. He could not articulate his devotion, but God understood. I told him to stop trying to read, to stop trying to make his body kneel and bow. I told him to look at an icon, to let his heart do the talking.

I told him that his spiritual life was better now than it had ever been before. He nodded vigorously. Oh, how that man had come to love God. "Play the music in your heart now," I said. "Play it in your heart." He clasped my hands, shaking and smiling.

We are so afraid of losing our abilities, our skills, our possessions. But to God all of that is nothing but trappings. To God, we are a heart, a soul, a being that is naked and beautiful, like a lily of the field. God has made us so exquisitely. I only have to look at a naked newborn baby in the hospital to know that. I come to bless the baby, but it is already blessed. God has made that child with such love. And that love will never diminish. It is always there.

Why do we worry so much when our heart and soul already belong to God? Why do we spend so much time struggling with the trappings of life when it is our core that will live forever? It is our soul that speaks, that sings. Spending time learning how to love—now that is time well spent. Jonathan left my office happy that day. He began gazing on an icon of the face of Christ. He later told me that his heart was able to play music with God.

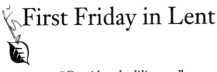

# First Friday in Lent

*"Consider the lilies . . ."*

LUKE 12:27

## The Beauty of the Self

We place fresh flowers on our altar at church each week. People donate the flowers in honor of loved ones, in memory of those that they loved who have died. They are beautiful, those flowers; each week brings a unique bouquet, spectacular in its own right.

It's strange how hard we are on ourselves. Few of us think of ourselves as beautiful. We tend to find ourselves repulsive, fat, ugly. We spend hours in front of our metaphorical mirrors, trying to eradicate whatever discrepancies we find staring us in the face.

"My thighs are too fat." "My nose is too large." I sometimes think that if we focused on an icon of Christ with the kind of time and intensity and focus that we give to our mirrors, we would be highly devout people. But instead we agonize about our own bodies, never realizing that a human being is not really designed to look at its own person. We were meant to find beauty in one another.

"Consider the lilies," Jesus said. God finds you beautiful just as you are, without the latest fashions or weight loss. God finds you beautiful because God made you so. God created you and found that you were very good. Not just good, but *very* good. Trust in that.

Our church secretary has a saying above her mirror. Every day, when she goes to the mirror to blow-dry her hair and apply her makeup, she reads this quotation: "You are beautiful in God's eyes." It has taken years of reading those words for them to begin to sink in, but she thinks that she is beginning to believe them.

Lilies grow effortlessly. The lilies in my backyard spread quickly, growing to easy heights, blowing their fierce colors in the wind. If God sees us as a flower, as a thing of effortless beauty, then we do well to remind ourselves of this perception every day. Every day we do well to remind ourselves that we are beautiful in God's eyes.

# First Saturday in Lent

*"And can any of you by worrying add a single hour to your span of life? . . . Consider the lilies . . ."*

LUKE 12:25–27

## The Antidote to Worry

I am a worrier. I think that I have worried all my life. I have struggled against this nature of mine, wondering what kind of marvelously productive things I could have accomplished if I hadn't spent so much time worrying. In the course of therapy, reading, and study, I have learned some things about worry and about the human mind.

Worry is nothing but a spinning of the wheels of the mind. It is an unproductive, unflattering waste of energy. Worrying is useless. I think that worrying for me is a way of trying to remain in control, of putting the brakes on my life. When I sit down to pray, the greatest distraction that faces me is worry. Worries can go around and around, resolving nothing, expending energy—a meaningless dance of distraction.

Most of us worry. We delude ourselves and call our worrying "processing." But deep inside we all know when we are processing and when we are just spinning our wheels.

It's strange of Jesus to suggest that the antidote to our worry lies in considering the simplest of things. A lily does not agonize over its decisions. It simply exists without judgment, without self-observation or consideration. A lily just is. It soaks in the sun and lives until the time comes for it to die.

I worried a lot about giving birth. I wanted to do it naturally, to experience everything. Yet my mind would fixate on the things that could go wrong, and I would worry. But that was before I had my first child. When the pain of labor began, I learned something tremendous. My body knew what it was doing. Even when my mind went crazy with fear or distraction, my body kept on doing what it was supposed to do. What was happening to me was like the rush of a river running its course. I did not need to worry; I was a part of a greater dance. And when the pain came, my mind stopped worrying. I suppose that I had better things to do with my time at that point. There was no room for worry, only room for me, my husband, God, and the someone else who was coming. Our baby was making its way into the world regardless of where my mind was at the time, and once I grasped this, I found it an immense relief.

Worrying does not add time to life, but rather robs us of it. When we worry, we are not fully awake. When we recognize that our thoughts are repeating themselves, when we go over and over the same problems, the same confusion or pain, we erase our presence from the moment. And we lose that moment, for it will never return.

I love how the lilies turn their faces to the sun. They arch their stems and find the light, wherever it may be. Consider the lilies of the field: leave your worries behind and turn to the Son.

# CHAPTER 2

# Seed

*A First Week in Lent*

# I Lent Sunday

*"A sower went out to sow his seed; and as he sowed, some fell on the path and was trampled on, and the birds of the air ate it up. Some fell on the rock; and as it grew up, it withered for lack of moisture. Some fell among thorns, and the thorns grew with it and choked it. Some fell into good soil, and when it grew, it produced a hundredfold."*

LUKE 8:5–8

## The Distribution

The islands of Hawaii were created in a remarkable movement of earth and sea. Mountains emerged from beneath the ocean as the earth shifted and settled. Birds then flew over the newly emerged land, leaving droppings filled with seed. Some of this seed must have fallen on rocky ground, but some fell on good soil and took root. Hawaii, to this day, is well known for its fruitful vegetation.

The seed is a powerful catalyst for growth. Inside that tiny, rock-hard pellet is life itself, enormous possibilities, trees, plants, fruit. Such a seed is the image that Jesus uses for the word of God. Jesus does not specify what kind of seed he is talking about here; perhaps that distinction does not matter. The same seed is poured out generously over everything, in the hope that it will take root and grow. The same word of God is offered to all people, for God tries to communicate with all of us. The variance is in our response, not in God's efforts.

I believe that God offers the same infinite love to all human beings. Yet our responses to God's love are as varied as the different soils of the parable. No matter where we are born on this planet, no matter how difficult or unimaginable our lives may be, God loves all of us the same. God pours down love like the rain, like the harvesting of seeds over a great spread of land. But the seed cannot penetrate a heart that is unreceptive. Instead it waits for receptivity.

Of course circumstances play a part in our spiritual lives. It is difficult for the seed of God's love to grow in the child who has been repeatedly abused—difficult, but not impossible. It is difficult for the seed to find a place to grow in a heart that has built up enormous defenses—difficult, but not impossible. Yesterday I was out jogging when I saw a flower that had grown out of the crack in a sidewalk. The seed of that flower had somehow found its way to the one opening in the pavement. And what might have seemed difficult was not impossible but beautiful.

The remarkable nature of a seed is that it simply makes itself available. If it cannot find a place to grow, it waits. Next season perhaps it will have better success at finding a chink in the armor, a place of warmth and moisture. If and when the seed lands in such a place, it brings forth new life.

The way that seeds blow in the wind, resting here and there, is like a cosmic dance of beauty. God showers the Divine self down upon us in myriad ways, and then waits to find a place to enter our hearts.

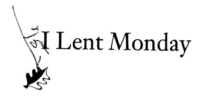

# I Lent Monday

## The Worn Path

Ground that has been trampled becomes compact, difficult to dislodge. There is no other way of adapting to the weight of feet pressing down upon it day after day.

As a child, I would hike down to a watering hole every day of the summer. The path along the way was worn hard by the shoes of the children traversing back and forth each day. Plants were trodden underfoot until they no longer grew. We could then see the way through the woods simply by following the compacted, mud-worn ground. This was the way to our swimming hole.

If a person is used over and over again, her soul can become flat and unreceptive to God's seed. Lucinda was this way. She had been raised to do her father's, and then her husband's, bidding, so at age seventy, she could no more identify her own needs than she could do magic. Asking her what she wanted was like asking a board to do cartwheels. She would just give me a blank stare. "I'll do whatever you want," she'd say.

I found myself urging Lucinda not to work in the kitchen at church all the time, but to sit still and let someone else wait on her. 'I don't like to do this," she'd say, "It makes me uncomfortable." That seemed to be an understatement. It wasn't just uncomfortable to her, it was intolerable. She was simply unable to think of herself as wanting or needing anything beyond the basic necessities of life.

Her husband continued the pattern by ordering her about, even in church. It bothered many people to see him trampling over her every Sunday, but he seemed unaware of his relationship with his wife. In his eyes she was created to do his bidding.

How do you convince a person that God loves them when they cannot even identify their own needs, when they cannot love themselves? It is a difficult prospect. When Lucinda's husband died, she was unable to remain alone. Within months she was married again, waiting on another man hand and foot.

And yet cracks do appear in sidewalks and seeds do grow. Maybe some seed will find a chink in that armor and Lucinda will feel that she is loved, even if she can't conceive of loving herself. I pray for her regularly; I pray that she will find her own heart under all that compacted dirt. Under all those "shoulds," there is a woman who wants and needs God's care and affection.

# 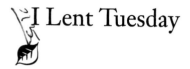I Lent Tuesday

## Rocky Soil

What exactly is rocky soil? Jesus later explains that those seeds that fell on rocky soil did spring up but then withered, for they had no moisture. Without moisture to draw up their roots, there was nothing to support them when the wind blew hard or the sun beat down. This was the shallow life of impulse and passion. They grew quickly and then burned up in the sun.

I have seen many seeds fall on rocky ground. One couple came to my church years ago. They were immediately taken with the service, the music, the preaching. "This is what I have been looking for all of my life!" Stuart would say. He would gush with compliments about my preaching, my teaching, claiming that his life was forever changed. He signed up for numerous activities at the church and soon was teaching teenagers, cleaning the church, and ushering at services. His attendance was terrific. In fact, he was so enthusiastic that he started calling me at home on my day off just to tell me that he found a great antique that would look great in our front hall. He seemed exorbitantly generous. There was no stopping his virulent devotion.

Then, one day, he didn't show up for a cleanup day at the church. "Where's Stuart?" everyone asked. He had become popular, and his charismatic presence was missed. I could not account for his absence, nor could I explain when I didn't see him for a good month. Finally I called him up.

"Donna and I have become totally absorbed in this antiquing!" he explained excitedly. "Of course, it eats up our Sundays, because if you are going to do it right, you have to devote the entire weekend, no holds barred. . . . But I'll be there this Sunday for sure! I wouldn't miss your services for anything, you know that!"

This time I was not as surprised when Stuart and his wife failed to show up on Sunday. I was not to see them for over a year. When they finally returned, they resumed complimenting me, but the words seemed hollow. Sure enough, they disappeared again for another year or so, and finally they stopped attending altogether, never fulfilling their promised commitments to the work of the church.

It is difficult to minister to those on spiritually rocky ground. Often they will jump into a church community with both feet. At first their development will seem rapid, almost bionic in its passion and commitment. And yet, despite their apparent passion and commitment, I often feel insecure about such people. Stuart and Donna, for example, often complimented me rather than speaking of God's role in their lives. Their words were generous and exorbitant, and yet Donna and Stuart had no depth to their understanding. When the work to which they had committed themselves began to mount, they simply withered and moved on to plant new seeds someplace else in their rocky soil. Presumably they have tried many forms of religiosity and none has ever stuck, for they did not know how to remain faithful when things were not new and exciting. Lacking deep spiritual roots, they never managed to make a true commitment to a faith practice and so they lived a flighty life of passion, charism, and eventual loneliness. Such is the life of someone rooted in rocky soil.

In gardening, the process of removing rocks from soil can be arduous. It takes enormous patience and is backbreaking work. Were Stuart and Donna to have enough self-awareness to recognize the pattern of their search for truth, they might want to pursue this kind of spiritual surgery, but I wonder whether they could have withstood the pain of it. Removal of the stones within their hearts would not only take an arduous therapeutic process, but would force them to recognize the shallow nature of their very selves. It is much less painful to simply move on to another passion, another focus. But I'm afraid that this makes for a lonely life of short-term relationships and an endless chasing after the wind.

# I Lent Wednesday

## The Thorns

She came to church faithfully, regularly, despite the busyness of college life. She found herself strangely moved in church, though she had grown up in a household of agnostics. "My father was too drunk to pray," she explained one Sunday at coffee hour. She had a bright smile, and claimed that she had found new freedom in her freshman year. "It's so good to be away from home," she'd say over and over again.

Debbie was a beautiful young woman: blond hair, blue eyes, great smile. Then, one Sunday morning, she came up to me in the receiving line after church. With a look of defiance, she announced, "Mother Kate, look what I did!" She stuck her tongue out to reveal a large, silver spikelike ornament that pierced the middle of her tongue. The area around the piercing looked irritated, possibly infected. "Oh," I gasped, "Well, that's a change!" I was at a loss for words. Was this just the latest fad in college, or was Debbie hurting herself?

Her troubles mounted. Debbie began to drop by my office unannounced. "I need to talk to you," she'd say. But then she would just sit on my sofa and squirm, unable to articulate her fears. Something was growing inside her and it was choking her.

One day I had an insight. "Debbie, did you pierce your tongue to stop yourself from telling me something?" Debbie looked up with fresh fear. "Yes, I believe that I did," she admitted.

Over the next few months, Debbie unveiled a story of enormous pain. It was a story of abuse, incest, violence, and alcoholism. She had enormous thorns that had grown up right along with her. But the process of extracting those thorns was deep and painful, and she sought the help of a psychiatrist. Not once but three times I visited Debbie in the psychiatric ward of a hospital, each time after she had tried to take her own life. During those visits she painted gruesome images of her pain and suffering. She was filled with fear and self-loathing.

How does one proceed when the word falls upon such thorns? Of course, these thorns were not of Debbie's own making. They were planted into her existence years and years ago. The only way that I knew to proceed was to try to help Debbie examine those thorns and, over time, find a way to maneuver around them. I wasn't sure that all of them could be extracted, but I did know that there was very little room for the word of God to grow in her heart until she contended with some of her demons.

For years Debbie has wrestled with her thorns. They have choked the normal development of her spiritual life and restricted her comprehension of God's love. But she is a woman of incredible tenacity, and I don't think that the thorns will have the last word in her life.

More often than not, these kinds of life-threatening thorns do choke the word of God. It is a reality. Some of us do not have Debbie's courage to face our demons. We find ourselves unable to experience the love and joy of God. Instead, our pain and past experiences choke the life-giving message of the Gospel, and we find ourselves existing alone with the thorns that have become so deeply embedded in our lives. Even if you do not have this struggle yourself, you know someone who does.

The environment in which a person lives does make an enormous difference in the growth of their spirit. Should the word of God fall among thorns, it is difficult for it to take root and grow. No matter how much such people are told that they are loved by God, they simply cannot experience that love fully. The love of God is pushed away, choked by the pain of their existence. And yet I can tell you that Debbie is slowly improving. After years of therapy, she has extracted some of those thorns. Others, she has learned to outmaneuver. She is alive, and she is finding patches of good soil in her heart.

# I Lent Thursday

## Good Soil

I see many people who have good spiritual soil. They come honestly searching for God. Over time they find God. They give of themselves, of their time and energy. They are enriched by the church community, by the worship, and I have the joy of watching them flower.

One family came to our church two years ago. They were not without their troubles. The mother and father were on the verge of a divorce, their daughters unable to communicate with their parents and failing in school. Yet they made a conscious decision as a family to come to our church. Every Sunday they came. One of the girls came to talk with me regularly. Both kids joined the youth group. The parents separated for a while, and then, with some therapy and much prayer, they moved back in together. The mother began to read about God, devouring much of my library. The father began to usher and to cook church breakfast on Sundays. Both were able to express their love of God in different ways. They found themselves more and more at home in the community. The kids also found themselves again and are happier, more joyful. One of them wants to become a priest.

Why was this family receptive to God's seed? I think it was because their soil was basically good. Each one of them wanted peace, each of them wanted to find God. All they needed was a little watering—a place to connect with community and to grow toward one another again.

I cannot tell you why some soil is good, just as I cannot predict how a plant will respond to new soil. The growth is up to God. But I do know a few ways in which we can prepare our spiritual soil.

*Water.* Find ways to nourish yourself. Ask yourself, What is it that feeds my soul? Once a week I like to wander the stacks of a bookstore and sip coffee. My friend needs to sing each day. My husband loves to exercise with intensity. Find the water that quenches your thirst. Many of us do not find enough time alone with ourselves, time to think, time to just be. Without the water to quench the thirsty soil of your soul, the seed of God's message cannot make itself at home.

*Fertilizer.* There is a balance to fertilizer. It is a chemical balance that I have not mastered. And yet I do know that having a particular mix of certain chemicals and minerals makes soil receptive to different kinds of plants, but you have to know the kind of plant that you wish to grow. You have to know what kind of balance would work best with your soil. So too do you have to discover who you are and what you need in order to be nourished.

*Patience.* Remember that growth does not happen instantaneously. When nonbelievers come to church, I ask them, "Are you willing to devote some *time* to the possibility of God's existence?" If they are willing to worship, to pray, to become part of the community, over time the seed will grow. But they must give it time. Belief will often follow regular practice. But we must be willing to take the time to let God work in our lives.

Just a few days ago, a woman brought me a bag of compost from her garden. This is the richest kind of soil, dark and luscious. And it was made from ashes, decomposed trash, and other inedibles! Sometimes living though a mess or two can make our soil rich. The family with whose story I opened today had been through a lot, but they were the richer for their struggles. They were ready for the seed to be planted in their hearts.

# I Lent Friday

*"For truly I tell you, if you have faith the size of a mustard seed, you will say to this mountain, 'Move from here to there,' and it will move; and nothing will be impossible for you."*

MATTHEW 17:20

## The Tiniest of Seeds

What is baptism? Why do we baptize babies when they cannot articulate their response to God? The best analogy I can come up with has to do with the planting of a seed.

When first I held a mustard seed in my hand, I couldn't believe how small and insignificant it seemed. It is dark brown, slim, and tiny. I could have easily let it slip through my fingers and it would have disappeared into the ground. How could I have found it again in the dirt? It would have blended in completely. I could plant it and see no visible change for many weeks. It was so tiny, I was inclined to believe that it must have been simply swallowed up by the ground. But in the midst of the earth, something was stirring in that tiny seed: the potential for enormous growth, enormous possibility.

It is the same with baptism. The child may sleep through the whole event. Even if she screams the entire time, she will no more remember her baptism than you and I can remember our first diaper being changed. But deep down in her soul, a seed will begin to grow.

And as that seed of God grows in her heart, we must approach her spiritual life as if it were a plant. We cannot expect too much too soon. We must nurture it gently, water it, give it time and nourishment. And as she grows, God will grow inside her heart.

"What should we do?" the godparents usually ask. "Tend the seed that we have planted in her heart. Water and nourish the plant," I reply. When she wants to be read stories about God from children's books, read to her. When she begins to ask questions about the nature of the divine and human suffering, answer to the best of your ability. Show her the beauty of God's creation and remind her who made all that. Find her passions, her talents, and remind her that they are gifts from God. Whenever there is an opening, bring God into the conversation. Watch her spiritual life grow, and nourish it as you would nourish a plant. Do not put too much stress on it when it is too young. Give it time to grow, and then ask much of it as it strengthens. Tend to her heart and her life with God.

It is a tall order, the calling of a godparent. Most of us don't do justice to that incredible privilege. What an honor to watch over the spiritual life of a child.

The mustard plant is difficult to raise. It must be watered in just the right way in order to thrive. But once it is thriving, it can grow to enormous proportions. We put a huge plant in our parish hall last week. No one could believe that it was a mustard plant. Strong, stocky leaves, coarse and weathered. A thick stem that grew to a great height. Who would have believed that such a small seed could grow so large? What immense possibilities we have as human beings if we give our spiritual lives time and nourishment.

# I Lent Saturday

*"Other seeds fell on good soil and brought forth grain, some a hundredfold, some sixty, some thirty."*

MATTHEW 13:8

## No Growth Chart

Once seeds hit good soil, production differs! The Master seems to celebrate all grain production, regardless of how much is grown. He notes the amount. Each grain is counted, each is valued, and yet all amounts are celebrated together. There is no competition once the word of God meets rich soil.

The clergy of our local churches met a few weeks ago to discuss our spiritual lives. After years of mere formalities and business discussions, we wanted to start supporting one another on a spiritual level. Strange that it took us so long. Even so, we all felt that we were taking a risk in sharing our prayer lives. Maybe, so we thought, maybe we did not experience God as much as the next guy. Maybe we would feel intimidated by one another. We soon found we had built up enough support to override these insecurities.

We started with a simple Bible study followed by a question about how we had each experienced God's call to the ordained ministry. This was a question that we had all answered before, for you cannot be ordained a priest in the Episcopal Church without responding to this question many times. To my surprise, many of us told of mystical experiences of God: dreams, visions, hearing God's voice. And yet others spoke of nothing but a settled feeling, or the affirmation of those around them.

I looked around the room. Who would have known that we were so different and so much the same? What a shame that we had spent years comparing attendance at our churches, as if the church with the most people were the one dearest to God. Clearly God was present, shining upon all of us and revealing the Divine self in many unique and beautiful ways.

How did we ever come to think that God might compare spiritual growth? The notion is completely foreign to Jesus' parables of the seeds. It is a twentieth-century notion, an industrial motivator. The creation of competition can increase production, or so we have come to believe. But this logic does not compute in the spiritual life. We are not businesses here, we are growing beings. We provide soil and God controls the growth. As long as we are receptive, the grain produced is worth celebrating, no matter its amount. God celebrates your growth as if you alone were in the universe, as if you alone mattered, as if every tiny particle of growth is a miracle of life itself, as if you are the whole universe wrapped up in one. The birth of your gifts, your time spent with God, your prayers, your service to God—it all is worth celebrating. Don't compare your spiritual life with those around you. God does not do that. You are unique and you are very good.

# CHAPTER 3

# Fruit

*A Second Week in Lent*

# II Lent Sunday

*"You will know them by their fruits."*

MATTHEW 7:16

## One-of-a-Kind Fruit

I stand in the cluttered kitchen, cutting up strawberries to take to a new mother. Our church brings meals for the first two weeks after a birth, to help the parents settle into life with a child without having to worry about food.

The strawberries are deep red, shot through with juices so sweet that I can smell them. I have to sample as I cut. Each strawberry produces a taste all its own. Some of the sweetest are those with bruises on the outside. Some of the most beautiful to look at taste sour.

Jesus uses the image of producing fruit numerous times throughout the Gospels. He does this in order to convey profound meaning about the nature of our relationship with God and with one another. Let us plumb the depth and richness of this metaphor.

All human beings produce something. Our behavior has ramifications, our decisions affect those around us. This is part of the nature of our universe. Every time we take a step, we change our universe. Everyone produces fruit of some kind.

Funerals are times when we reflect on the fruit of a human life. And it is so easy to recognize a person who has loved God. No matter what religion they practiced, a godly person will have impacted the world in some way. People will come out of the woodwork to express their love for this person. Stories will be told of service to the world, of a person who inspired others, of someone who gave something back to us. Often the people at the funeral will hear of fruit that they never knew about: they will hear how the man who died gave money to the poor, how he inspired his daughter, or how he loved to sing. "I never knew that!" they will say. "I never knew that he did so much for others."

The taste of each strawberry is slightly different from the next. In fact, as with all fruit, no two strawberries are exactly alike. If you look closely, you can see that each one is unique. Each was created in a slightly different environment. One might have blossomed on a hot day, another on a day with a slight breeze. No two came about in exactly the same way. No two rest at the exact same place on the stem. No two are exactly alike.

My six-year-old son is just entering first grade. Even this early in life, he is frequently asked, "What do you want to be when you grow up?" Most of these questions are from adults attempting to be friendly, to find something to talk about. Yet Americans are so bent on productivity that we program our children to be channeled into a career, never stopping to realize that they have unique paths to self-expression. The fruit of one soul cannot be packaged along with other fruit. No two are alike. We simply cannot mass produce the goals of a lifetime. No wonder my son Luke can never answer that question with just one path. "I want to be a fireman-geographer-astronaut," he says. And I smile. Yes, I think, your path will be your own, and your fruit will taste like no one else's. It will be your unique gift to the world.

What freedom comes with the realization that you are unique! God does not expect you to model your life on the achievements of another. God calls you to trust in the unique qualities of your spiritual fruit. No one can duplicate that which God calls for you to be. Just like the strawberry, you are one of a kind. Explore your own forms of self-expression with the knowledge that no one else will be able to do it your way.

# II Lent Monday

*"Every tree that does not bear good fruit is cut down and thrown into the fire."*

MATTHEW 7:19

## The Essence of Fruit

Sometimes I find myself wondering about the absurdity of worship. Why do I breathe more easily the moment I set foot in a church? Why do I spend my life prancing around a beautiful building in robes, singing and trying to interpret the Bible for people? Why do I pass the bread around? And why in the world do I find it all so meaningful? To the outsider it must look like a great show. Why does all this ceremony mean so much to me?

Last Sunday was one of those down summer Sundays. Attendance was just short of normal. People seemed sleepy. In an effort to give myself some time off, I had invited another priest to preach. He did an awful job, reading lines of sixteenth-century poetry that no one could hear, let alone understand. The PA system failed, and left an eerie buzzing but no amplification. The singer got sick at the last minute. Because everyone was on vacation or had just overslept, we were left with just one acolyte who had never before carried the cross. He keep looking back to make sure that we were all following. The whole thing was just off, sloppy. I arrived home contending with that darned old worry that creeps up in the down times: What the heck am I doing with my life?

I don't think you can be a priest in this day and age and not awaken to the absurdity of your actions from time to time. The fact is, we are doing something that, based solely on outward appearances, looks ridiculous. We are miming an encounter with God and hoping that God does in fact show up. With no way to verifiably measure God's presence, we are left hoping that we are not just playing the fool.

A friend of mine who is an artist says that she feels more alive during the creation of a painting than at any other moment in her life. She really feels that the process of painting somehow reinvigorates the core of her being, and if she cannot paint, she is somehow diminished. I feel the same way about the liturgy of the Church. If nothing else, it reinforces my very self.

I found a raspberry bush deep in the woods this summer.

The birds seemed to have left this bush alone; perhaps they had not found it due to its remote location and all the overgrowth of trees around it. I looked at the berries, ripe and luscious on their branches. Why did this bush produce fruit in the middle of nowhere, in an area where neither man nor beast would visit? It produced fruit because of its very nature.

Jesus instructs us to bear fruit with an urgency that is unprecedented. It is not just asked of us; God requires that we bear fruit. The tree that does not bear fruit is cut down and thrown into the fire. Though this passage is disturbing, it does convey the absolutely essential nature of our bearing fruit. We simply must find a way to bear fruit or we are denying the essence of our nature. If we live our entire lives without bearing fruit, we are hollow shells of human beings: there is nothing left in us that is truly individual, truly eternal.

I may never fully understand why the Eucharist moves me so deeply. Maybe I am not capable of fully understanding. My job is just to get on over to the church, to write my sermons, and to distribute the bread of Christ. It may seem absurd at times, and it may appear meaningless in the low times, but it is my fruit. It is simply who I am.

# II Lent Tuesday

*"Thus you will know them by their fruits."*

MATTHEW 7:20

## The Taste of Fruit

The outer appearance of a fruit does not necessarily coincide with its inner taste and richness. Some of the best tasting fruit does not look so good, and some of the worst tasting is beautiful on the outside. So it is with the gifts of the spirit. God does not speak in a language of appearances. As Jesus said, God looks upon the heart.

Bananas are a great example. The best bananas are a bit worn, bruised, aged. These are soft and sweet, the best for a banana cream pie or a milk shake. When my baby, Max, was tiny, I found that the oldest, most worn-out looking bananas were perfect for his tiny mouth, soft enough to be mashed by his gums, sweet as candy. I think that his first word came at six o'clock one morning when he looked at me, his mouth full of banana, and said, "Mmmm."

Fruit teaches us a lesson about the relationship between outward appearances and the life of the spirit. Not all beautiful fruit tastes bad. Not all old fruit is good. If a fruit is too battered and bruised, we know that it will not be pleasing to the taste. But we simply cannot rely on the outward appearance of fruit. We can't find out what it's really like until we cut it open and look upon the heart.

You may think that the year you spent working on a book that was never published was wasted time. But how do you know that? Yes, by outward standards, very little was accomplished, but what became of your heart? Did you grow closer to God that year? Were you home to smile at your daughter when she arrived from school? How do you know what that fruit might have tasted like to God? This kind of thinking can change our concept of failure. We will not fully know the taste of our fruit until we meet our Maker and sit down at the banquet table in the kingdom of heaven.

Understanding this metaphor also helps us not to judge others so quickly. Sometimes the outward appearance of a man does not do justice to his character. And sometimes the most polished person later disappoints. One of the greatest artists in my congregation is a man who is nearly homeless. He suffers from schizophrenia. He won't take his medications because he claims that it dampens his creativity. He seems to change his thoughts in the middle of a sentence. He wears tattered clothes and he smells. But he can make a sculpture of angels that takes my breath away. Though outwardly he looks lost, inwardly he holds a lot of richness.

# II Lent Wednesday

> *"No good tree bears bad fruit, nor again does a bad tree bear good fruit; for each tree is known by its own fruit."*

LUKE 6:43

## Looking at the Tree

I know a woman who worries all the time. She occasionally comes to talk to me in my office. "Every day I ask God to forgive me," she says. When I ask her why she feels that she has wronged God, she cannot say why. When pressed, she comes up with small mistakes, items left undone, difficult judgment calls.

"I do not see why these things would anger God," I'll explain. "After all, you are trying to do your best."

"Yes," she replies, "but my best isn't good enough."

This woman suffers from a kind of inbred anxiety that is difficult to identify and still more difficult to eradicate. As a young child, she was told that she was too abrasive, too bossy, too loud. And so she began to censure herself, to cast judgment upon her every decision. And in a world where we can only do our best, she is constantly able to find fault with herself. Her prayers, asking God to forgive her all the time, show her inability to know herself as a good person. Her true sin is her lack of belief in her own goodness.

How do you convince a person of their innate goodness? It is only those who are genuinely kind and considerate who worry about their actions. The very fact that they are concerned with their decisions makes them conscientious and capable.

On the flip side, I have met people who constantly seem to hurt others and yet have no awareness of the destructive pattern of their lives. "I've had such abusive relationships," one woman explained to me. And yet, just weeks later, she came to me, excited about moving to another city with a man whom she had just met. "He's everything that I've been looking for. . . . Good-bye!" I just knew that this relationship, like all the others, would end up with her fleeing just as quickly as she had fallen in love. Jobs, houses—all seemed to change constantly for her. She had lived in more cities in the past ten years than I had in a lifetime. And yet she was unable to reflect upon the fact that this life of constant attraction and rejection was the fruit of her troubled nature.

In a way, the best kind of therapeutic process takes a look

at the tree rather than its fruit. When a good counselor sees a pattern in a person's life, the question is, What happened to the tree itself? Dwelling on the consequences of numerous failures in life will not address the real issue—why is this person failing over and over again?

Each tree is known by its fruit, Jesus says. How can you tell the inner workings of a soul? By looking at the pattern of behavior in a person's life. Despite radically difficult circumstances, a good soul will search for goodness and truth. A destructive person, even if given all the gifts of a bountiful life, will choose a pattern of blame and brokenness.

How do I convince this anxious woman that her fruits are good? I will assure her over and over again, but, in the end, it is God who will convince her of her worth.

# II Lent Thursday

*"For each tree is known by its own fruit."*

LUKE 6:44

## The Gift of Consumption

Fruit is meant to be eaten. Why else would God have made it taste so good? It is meant to be devoured by someone in order to spread the seeds far and wide.

The fruit of the spiritual life is also meant to be consumed by others. We become most fulfilled when our spiritual fruits feed those around us. It makes us grow. It promotes the kingdom of God.

When hurricane Katrina swept through the Gulf region, it left so much devastation. The people in my congregation wanted to help but didn't know how. One couple in particular called me over and over again, hoping to let some evacuees stay in their rental home. When I finally located a young couple who had been displaced by the hurricane, these parishioners were overjoyed. They came to church on Sunday smiling from ear to ear, because someone was going to consume their fruit. Someone could benefit from their goodness. And their goodness was spreading the kingdom of heaven. The evacuees could not believe that someone could be so generous. They began to come to church to see what this God thing was all about.

Fruit can reproduce even if it is not eaten but just left to rot. But if you want to spread the seeds far and wide, it is better for the fruit to be consumed. Letting your fruit be consumed is the finest way of ensuring that more will be produced, more seeds planted.

# II Lent Friday

*"Either make the tree good, and its fruit good; or make the tree bad, and its fruit bad; for the tree is known by its fruit."*

MATTHEW 12:33

## Finding Your True Fruit

How do I identify my fruit? Spiritual fruit must be something that communicates the essence of the soul—and thus of God—and spreads that essence out into the world. Your fruit is about sharing who you are in a genuine way. Your fruit is produced when you are true to yourself as made in God's image.

The problem is that so many of us get caught up in the expectations of others that we cannot find our true fruit. College students struggle with this web of expectations. Often they cannot identify their true gifts because the voices of parental expectation crowd out their true nature.

One of my best friends in college was an art history major. Janet loved art with a passion. She would spend hours pouring over paintings. "Look at this!" and she would explain how the artist's personality was expressed in the medium of a painting. She excelled in the field of art history, and she genuinely loved it.

In our junior year, her father became sick. A malignant tumor was expanding in his brain. They shaved his head. He came to pay her what would be his final visit to her dorm room. "Do something worthwhile with your life," he told her that evening as we sat together in her room. "Art history is fun, but it has no future. Get practical." He died one month later.

Janet's father had been a lawyer. That year, the light in her eyes began to dim and she began to apply to law schools. "Janet," I pleaded with her, "law is not what you love!" "But my dad was right," she said, "I have to do something more practical." I have not heard from her in years. She has disappeared into a big-city law firm.

I think that her father's expectations, coupled with his death, left Janet unable to produce her spiritual fruit. She was left producing his fruit instead. The last time I spoke to her, she was stressed out, overweight, and unhappy. If only she had the courage to find herself again.

If the fruit that we produce is not a true expression of our joy, of our very self, then it will drain us. True fruit should invigorate, it should bring about new life, a spreading of the essence of the self. When we produce our fruit of the soul, we should feel as if we have given away a piece of ourselves, and yet, miraculously, there is more and more of that self to share with others—more and more and more. Anything that diminishes the soul is not true fruit; it is an imitation, sapping life and vitality, and taking a piece of us with it.

# II Lent Saturday

*"My Father is glorified by this, that you bear much fruit and become my disciples."*

JOHN 15:8

## Ripening

We are waiting for strawberries to ripen in our backyard garden. My son Jacob goes out back frequently, "Mom!" he'll shout out, "What's taking them so long?" "It takes God some time to ripen a fruit," I'll explain. "Just wait. It will happen. But we can't pick it too soon; we have to let it grow. . . . Here, let's water them a bit more."

And so our ritual repeats itself. He asks why it's taking so long, I respond, and together we water. But deep down inside, I am wondering too: Why *does* it take so long to grow spiritual fruit?

I visited an elderly woman in the hospital. Her son sat by her bedside as she recovered. He told me of his life as a top executive, a lay leader of his church, a father and husband. He was happy, well, and very generous with his mother. "You have quite a son," I said. "I know," she replied with a smile. "And you know, he was the wildest kid. He locked his grandmother in the basement! He ran away from home. People said that he'd never amount to much. He decided he didn't want to go to college . . . but somehow, deep down inside, I knew that he was something special. He just had to develop in his own way. He couldn't be rushed." Thank God for the rare breed of parent who allows their child to develop at their own pace. This mother had given her son the greatest gift of all: she believed in him, and she nurtured him as his spiritual fruit grew at its own pace.

We have allowed ourselves to be seduced by the sin of busyness. We value speed almost above all else. Speed is money, speed is time. Speed is the best, the wave of the future, the new era. Fast food, fast service, fast everything. One woman had a heart attack in her car because she was so stressed out by a traffic jam. When we become this busy, we have no time to grow and develop.

There is an important process in the development of a fruit. It is called ripening. It is also an essential component of spiritual growth. One cannot rush the life of the spirit, just as one cannot make the strawberry plant produce faster. We must learn to wait for the ripening of the spirit.

Whenever the Church succumbs to the temptation of fast-production spirituality, we cheapen the depth of God's presence. You can have great music, masterful preaching and vivid art, but without patience, God may never show up.

"How does communion work?" one newcomer asked. "Does it change you immediately?" "Well, yes and no." I replied. "In your baptism a seed is planted. As you receive communion, that seed is nurtured. Like water dripping on a rock, communion will shape your entire being, but it is not a surgical procedure. It is a spiritual one. Give yourself time to grow with God."

The ripening of fruit is wholly out of our control. All that we can do is provide a nurturing environment. But God must change the essence of that fruit to make it ready for consumption. And what good is a fruit that is not ripe? It has no sweetness. Better to wait for those strawberries.

When we finally found a strawberry ripe and ready on the vine, Jacob danced for joy. I think he valued that little strawberry more than any fruit he had ever eaten. Its value had increased in the waiting.

**CHAPTER 4**

# Vine

*A Third Week in Lent*

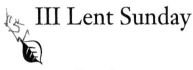# III Lent Sunday

*"I am the vine, you are the branches."*

JOHN 15:5

## The Will of God

A Roman Catholic priest was once asked what it was like to hear the confession of nuns. He thought for a moment, and then smiled. "It's like being bombarded by popcorn," he said.

Even nuns find something to confess. But this priest explained that much of their confessions have to do with a misunderstanding of the concept of following God's will. They feel that they have chosen their own will instead of God's will. This misunderstanding causes them much grief and guilt.

Even the most devout Christians fall into the trap of misunderstanding what it means to follow God's will. We assume that God has only one path in mind and that it's up to the devout to discern that one path and then follow it to its logical conclusion. In other words, God wants one decision, one left turn, one commitment at a time. The process of trying to discern this one true path causes enormous consternation. It's as if we are playing a guessing game with God. With every choice, with every dilemma, we must find out what God would have us do. The prospect of finding God's will takes enormous time and energy. There is a constant fear that we might get it wrong.

Years ago a faithful woman came to my office. She was nearly in tears. "I'm afraid to follow God's will," she explained to me. "I'm afraid that God will call me to go to Africa, but I don't want to go to Africa. I love my job and my life here. I'm deathly afraid of bugs and diseases!" She was distraught, convinced that her selfishness was preventing her from following God's will. She thought that God would call everyone to end starvation in Africa. It was the only path for true and faithful Christians. She was saying no to God's will for her life.

God's will is not a problem to be solved. It is not a guessing game. There is not just one answer to the question of the direction of your life. Instead of approaching the will of God as if it were a multiple-choice exam, I want us to return to the imagery that Jesus used. God does not administer standardized testing. There is no predetermined answer to the question of the will of God. In the fullness of the Divine, in the many dimensions of time and space, there is much more freedom. It is, in fact, possible to follow God's will and to be yourself at the same time.

Think of a vine. The vine is a remarkable plant that adapts itself to its surroundings. If a vine finds itself next to a rock, it will cover the rock. If it finds itself adjacent to a steep wall, it will grow at a ninety-degree angle. A vine has so many different directions in which it can flourish. It is known for its versatility and strength. The branches of the vine can grow in so many different directions, as long as they remain rooted in the stem. If Christ is the vine and we are the branches, then there is enormous freedom within the will of God. God celebrates the possibilities that are before you. God asks you to grow fiercely and freely, but to always remain rooted in the stem of God's being.

If we are the branches of a vine, then perhaps the question that we ought to ask ourselves is not, "Is this particular decision God's will?" but instead, "Is this decision rooted in Christ?" Does this decision naturally proceed forth from my love of God? Are my actions continuations of my life of faith? Are they firmly rooted in God? Within the framework of these new questions is enormous freedom and much less fear.

The vine is an incredible image that can re-form our relationship with God. We are free to grow in so many different directions, just as the vine grows—as long as we remain connected to the stem, to God. There are so many possibilities. Decisions become liberating when seen like this.

God wants you to be yourself. God celebrates the world that forms you and the choices that lie before you. Grow. Find yourself, your voice, your particular direction. But always remain rooted in the stem, in Christ, who is the core of your being.

Amen.

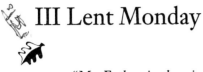

# III Lent Monday

*"My Father is the vinegrower. He removes every branch in me that bears no fruit. Every branch that bears fruit he prunes to make it bear more fruit."*

JOHN 15:1–2

## Intertwining

In our backyard is a vine that has grown so thick that it can hardly produce leaves. It needs to be cut back, trimmed, and its branches separated if it is to grow. It is difficult to push even one of my fingers into the morass that this vine has become. I cannot distinguish between its branches. Though it looks all right from a distance, up close I can see that its branches are so crowded that they are rotting.

Just like the vine, human beings can become too inter-twined. This kind of human crowding damages the spiritual life. Parents that do not release their children from their needs and demands can prevent that child from the kind of mental and spiritual growth that is necessary to live a full life. Such enmeshment stunts spiritual growth. Entire lives are lived within the small confines of parental expectation. If confined to a small space forever, the branches of the vine not only cannot grow, they begin to rot.

I rushed back to church one day to meet with a family. The mother had died suddenly. Her two grown boys and her husband were shocked and unstable. Though the church surrounded them in their grief, they were at a loss as to how to live without this woman. She had, quite literally, dominated their lives.

We sat down for an hour session. In preparation for all funerals, I meet with the family to listen to their stories about the deceased. This not only is therapeutic for the newly bereaved, but also helps me to prepare a sermon. Often a gospel message is hidden in the life of the one who died.

But this session was a surprise. This woman had been a long-standing, faithful parishioner. She was greatly loved by many in the church. Expecting to have a cathartic time of crying and release, I was taken aback when the family was unable to express its grief. The boys were so consumed with unresolved issues that they spent most of the hour talking about themselves. When I pressed them to tell me stories about their mother, they returned again and again to the ways that their lives were incomplete. "I never could marry," one of them said. "No one was ever good enough for mother. . . . But maybe she would have accepted someone over time. . . ." The other son spoke of how his mother had prevented him from moving to Alaska after college. "Just when I was free and brave enough to go," he said, "we had a knock-down fight. She just laid down the law. . . . I ended up moving home."

These men were in pain not because their mother had died but because she had stunted their growth. Their lives were controlled by their mother. She had crowded them, holding them back from finding out who they really were.

After the shock and grief of her death, one of the sons began to grow into the newly found freedom that he had been given. He found happiness with a woman. He moved away. The other, somehow more incapacitated than his brother, did not grow into the emptiness but remained stunted, living in memory, telling the same stories over and over again at coffee hour for years.

Once a vine has become so densely intertwined, there is no way to trim it without forceful cutting. I will have to simply cut out a hole in the dense area. It may feel at the time as if I am cutting out the heart of the plant, surgically removing some of its insides. But after the process is over, the healthy branches of the vine that remain will have room to grow once more.

# III Lent Tuesday

*"Just as the branch cannot bear fruit by itself unless it abides in the vine, neither can you unless you abide in me."*

JOHN 15:4

## The Connection

A few days ago, I did an experiment. I tried to cut a few branches from the vine in my backyard. I put them in a vase full of clean, clear water. Within days they were dead. They withered without the nourishment that comes from the stem of the vine. I tried the experiment again, even putting sugar in the water. The branches lived a little longer, but eventually they withered and died. I could not replicate the life force that came to them from the stem of the vine. Cutting them off from the stem meant gradual depletion and death.

Time and time again, people who are withering on the vine come to me. One man was in his fifties, was working endless hours in corporate America, and was profoundly depressed.

"I do not see the purpose of my life," he said. "Every day I work ungodly hours for this company, and yet if I left, they would simply find a replacement. I go to bed at night, having exhausted my body and mind, but with no sense that my work has mattered to anyone. Why do I keep on living? I am so afraid to tell my wife how unhappy I am. She has no idea. I am all alone." This man had been cut off from the meaning of his life. He was spending his time generating income without passion, without connection. The result was a gradual withering of his very self. He was so unhappy that he was considering suicide.

Accepting a job because of pay without regard for its meaning, moving to a new location for convenience when your heart belongs in another place, telling a falsehood because "it just seemed easier"—all of these are ways in which we gradually become cut off from the core of our being, from our passion, from Christ. The results are never instantaneous, but they are always the same: a withering of the soul.

People sometimes ask me how I can burden people by asking them to volunteer in the church. "Don't you feel guilty when you ask a busy father of four to work in the church painting a wall on a Saturday? Doesn't the man already have enough to do? Is it so pastoral to burden him with additional tasks?"

On the surface, it does look like I am asking this man to do more, to get even busier. But time and time again, I have watched as this kind of man finds deep joy in his work at the church. I have watched as factory workers found themselves reconnected to meaning, to a purpose. "I am so tired at the end of the week," one man said to me. "But coming to church and shoveling dirt with other parishioners feeds my soul. I can't explain it; I just feel happier." The Church can provide a connection to the vine that is Christ. Another woman told me that if she does not come to worship on Sunday morning, her week feels somehow disconnected. She becomes drained, tired.

Just yesterday I visited an elderly woman who is grieving the death of her husband. They lived in a loving marriage for over forty years. Now that he is gone, she rattles around the house alone. "I am sleeping all day, and I lie awake most of the night," she told me. "I know that I need to get out, but I am just so tired." I suggested that she come to church and answer the telephone during the afternoon hours when she is prone to sleeping. "Oh, I can't do that. . . . I'm just too tired." I left unable to persuade her that by reentering the community of Christ, she would be reinvigorated. Instead, she is choosing to remain alone, withering on the vine.

Finding meaning in one's life, being of service to others—

this is life-generating stuff. Give a person a purpose, a reason for living, and you give that person life itself. God has a unique purpose for each of us, a reason why we are alive. If we lose touch with that core of our being, we will wither on the vine. No amount of sugar in the water will suffice. There is simply no replacement for genuine meaning in life.

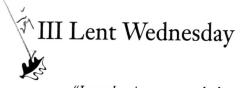

# III Lent Wednesday

*"I am the vine, you are the branches."*

JOHN 15:5

## Growing through the Cracks

There is a vine that has crept through our air-conditioning unit and into the house. It reaches into our sunroom like some long lost finger from Eden. I asked a gardener about how it got inside. "Oh," he said with a smile, "the vine is an amazing plant. I have watched vines destroy stone walls. Just give it time and, if left unchecked, that vine will take down your house. It will start by covering the walls, then work its way through brick and mortar until the structure crumbles. Of course all of this takes hundreds of years, but just give it time. It is an amazing plant."

If Christ is the vine and we are the branches, then the life of faith is a lot stronger than we realize. The spiritual life is much more persistent, much more resilient than we can possibly imagine. If cut back or hurt, it will grow back if we give it time.

We were walking back to the car. Wounded in Vietnam, Tom needed a walker to make his way to his car, but the walker kept getting caught on the vines that grew beside the house. "Damn those vines!" he cursed under his breath. "I can't seem to get loose of them!" They seemed to cling to him as he shuffled across the walk. "Why don't they let me go?" he laughed.

Tom was a Vietnam veteran. Half of his platoon was killed. He came back from the war an atheist, driven to drinking and depression. He vowed never to let God into his heart.

But there had been a moment in the middle of the fiercest battle in Nam. It was just before dawn; he was stoned and had been fighting all night. He was frantically shooting all around, fighting an unseen enemy that could kill him at any instant. Bullets seemed to be flying all around him. He was mad with terror.

And then something happened. He stopped shooting. There was silence, a silence impenetrable, deep, and rich. The rising sun filtered through the leaves of the trees, and he thought, "Why am I here?"

Within seconds the fighting resumed. But that moment wouldn't leave my friend Tom. As much as he stayed stoned and drunk, that moment would creep up on him, reminding him of this gentle presence.

He returned from Nam determined that he didn't believe in anything. For two decades he struggled to stay afloat, fighting alcoholism and depression. Finally, one day, he found himself wandering into a Quaker meeting. "And there it was," he would later tell me, "the silence that I had heard so long ago in the jungle. It was still there, waiting for me. Without my knowing it, God had found a way into my heart."

Don't underestimate the power and resilience of a true vine. It will wind its way into your life and never let go.

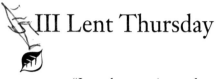

# III Lent Thursday

*"I am the true vine, and my Father is the vinegrower."*

JOHN 15:1

## Prayer Grows in Many Directions

If Christ is the vine, living within us, then our life of prayer can grow as a vine grows. That means that there is no one right way to pray! If a vine can grow over, under, around, and through the many objects it encounters, so Christ can relate to us in many and varied ways. You need not force yourself to sit down and read the Bible for an hour each evening if that seems difficult and unproductive. The vine can grow in so many circumstances. Try praying in the car. My friend calls these windshield prayers. Try singing to God in the shower. Try visiting a museum and witnessing the light of God in paintings. There is no one right way to pray.

It is amazing to me how much guilt is associated with prayer. Many people find themselves unable to do the kind of formal prayer that they read about in Church history books.

A professor of science once lamented his inability to pray. "I read all day long," he said. "At night I try to drag out the *Book of Common Prayer* and do the daily office readings from Scripture, but my mind just won't focus. I am saturated with words. I feel so bad. I am failing at prayer." What he was failing at was not prayer, but reading. I suggested that he try sitting in front of an icon. He found this much more rewarding, and he was able to feel God's presence with him in a few moments without words.

Prayer can adapt to the circumstances of our lives. One woman paints to pray. She finds that color springs from her fingertips into new expression. God is vivid to her in this way. Another man sings in a community choir. The sacred music makes his soul sing to God. Many people will come to me wishing that they prayed more, but when we examine their lives, we often find that they have been praying for years, just not in the way that they expected. I found deep communion with God when I nursed my baby. Simply rocking him by the open window, watching the autumn leaves fall. I had never felt such peace.

Do we think that God can relate to us only in the written word, in the Sunday sermon? Christ finds his way into our hearts in the smallest of seconds, in the smile of a loved one, in a dance. He is as versatile as the vine, growing into our hearts almost imperceptibly, finding his way into the core of our being, waiting for us to notice that he has been there all along.

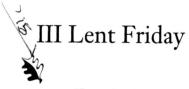

# III Lent Friday

*"I am the vine, you are the branches."*

JOHN 15:5

## Seasons of the Spirit

The vine has periods of enormous growth and periods of dormancy. All plants follow this pattern according to the seasons. Growth usually does not happen at a steady, even pace all year. There are seasons of growth and seasons of rest, seasons of cold and seasons of warmth. So it is with the life of the spirit.

We are often unable to give ourselves permission to have a period of dormancy. Sometimes God just doesn't feel so close to us. Sometimes life appears humdrum and routine. Sometimes the mystical component seems to be absent, and we find ourselves flat and uninspired. This is a natural part of the spiritual experience. Any organic growth process must have periods of rest and inactivity. Growth never occurs consistently, but rather in waves, in seasons. And these waves of growth are beyond our control.

The vine can grow tremendously one season, then not grow at all. Like the growth of a human child, the vine seems to expand in seasonal spurts.

One day I woke up and my third baby boy had become a toddler. Did this happen overnight? No, but he had had a growth spurt. Part of the growth had to do with my perception, part had to do with his true growth spurt. But the fact is that he grew rapidly in one fell swoop, and surprised his mom one morning.

Periods of rapid spiritual growth are exciting. We welcome the passion, the connection that we feel with God. We believe that we have finally tapped into the source of our inspiration. When the spiritual connection fades or slows down, we wonder why God has left us. We fail to understand the spiritual life as a vine. The vine has not stopped its development. It has simply reached a different season. There are also seasons of the soul.

And, just as with a vine, spiritual growth can be stalled, even damaged, by harsh conditions. Too much heat, wind, or fire can damage the vine. Our spiritual lives are not immune to damage. We are living beings who respond to circumstances around us. If you have lost a loved one to death, you may enter a period of serious spiritual dormancy, doubt, and even despair. Your vine will one day grow again, but it must be watered, nurtured, brought back to life. Give it time and gentle attention. A strong vine will grow once more when the season is right. But we must allow ourselves the time to rest, reflect, and open our hearts to the possibility of new growth.

If a vine has been damaged, say, by a fire or an obstacle, it will often grow back in a new and alternative direction. If you have been hurt, do not expect yourself to emerge as the same person who suffered loss once. You will grow again, but your growth may take new and unexpected directions.

So it is with the spirit. The branches of the vine may grow again, but they may grow in a new area that was once altogether unexplored. Be open to new possibilities and give yourself permission to rest.

# III Lent Saturday

*"I am the true vine, and my Father is the vinegrower. He removes every branch in me that bears no fruit. Every branch that bears fruit he prunes to make it bear more fruit."*

JOHN 15:1–2

## Pruning

The process of pruning is known throughout the gardening world. Even amateurs like me know that to cut back the branches of a bush makes the bush come in thicker. Pruning can help trees to produce fruit, flowers to bloom, health to be abundant. In other words, less is sometimes more in the spiritual life.

When is it time to cut back? When must we admit that things have grown a bit out of hand? When is it time to prune the vine of our spiritual lives?

Last week I got a call from a faithful parishioner who was struggling with her overcommitment to the church. "I have to back out of the Capitol Campaign Committee," she said. I could hear the guilt resounding in her voice. "I'm so sorry, but I am doing so much that I don't feel I have time for God. . . . I don't want to feel burdened by my service at the church. . . . Is this okay with you?"

This woman expected a scolding. But in reality she was doing exactly what she needed to do. The most faithful, dedicated parishioners will inevitably be asked to do many things in the church. It is important that they learn to prune back the branches of their spiritual reach. If they succumb to the pressure to stretch themselves, to cover every task, they will suffer.

How do you know when its time to prune back your branches? Sometimes, as in Jesus' words above, God does it for you. Many branches have been pruned back when the body fails us: inevitable heart attacks, loss of energy, even depression can cause people to stumble and to reevaluate their lives. Sometimes these cataclysmic events give us a much-needed message—that we must slow down or die. It is impossible to bear fruit for God if we are stretched too thin.

So I told my faithful parishioner that she was taking care of herself, that what she was doing was right, even though it was hard. I told her that not only was I not disappointed, I was pleased. For she was choosing to prune back her branches so that she could experience the grace of God again in her life.

# CHAPTER 5

# Harvest

*A Fourth Week in Lent*

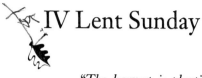 IV Lent Sunday

> *"The harvest is plentiful but the laborers are few; therefore ask the Lord of the harvest to send out laborers into his harvest."*

MATTHEW 9:37–38

## Laborers

I stood in a crowded airport in the Caribbean. The air conditioning was not working. Five flights were delayed. The air in the room was stale. The place was packed with sunburned, disgruntled people waiting for flights that should have left long since. People were tired, hungry, and grumpy. "Why can't they fix the air-conditioning?" one man loudly complained to his wife. When a flight was announced, people would jostle themselves in line, ignoring the eyes of the old man who found himself elbowed out of place.

The crowds surrounding Jesus had traveled for days. They were hungry, unsure of where they would sleep that night. Blindly they had followed him in the hope that they might be able to touch him, catch a glimpse of his face, hear his words. They were, as Jesus describes, "harassed and helpless, like sheep without a shepherd" (Matthew 9:36).

Jesus looked out over the sea of faces, and he saw immense opportunity. He saw the potential for souls to come to God. Using imagery from nature, he compared the crowd to a harvest.

When Jesus looked out over the crowds, he saw the abundance of a harvest. Jesus saw ripe and ready souls and immense opportunities for bringing these souls to God. If only there were people to reap the harvest, workers to simply bring in the sheaves.

Even today, the work of the Church, if honestly and faithfully presented, is bountiful. People are hungry to talk with a priest, hungry to ask questions, eager to worship and curious as to how to find inner peace. But the situation today is the same as it was then: who is going to do the ministry? There are never enough laborers.

Being a laborer does not entail a seminary education. It does not mean that you have to exhaust yourself with selfless work twenty-four hours a day. It does not mean that you have to give up your secular job or join a monastery. It means that you are willing to be present with people, with God in mind.

The television show *Joan of Arcadia* presented a remarkable episode about a teenage girl who sees God. God appears to Joan in her high school and asks her to ask a boy to the upcoming dance. The boy's name is Ramsey. He is a disturbed boy who is prone to bursts of anger. He is a social outcast, overweight, and awkward. He is full of hatred.

Joan has a wonderful way of arguing with God. "Who are you kidding?" she says, "What you're talking about is social suicide!" But she obeys, asking the boy out on a date. He is so surprised that, at first, he doesn't believe her. But he agrees. The next day she brings him a tie, crumpled in her pocket. "Here," she says, "wear this to the dance."

Their night together is a disaster. Ramsey brings a bottle of whiskey. Joan tells him to put it away, and he does, but the teachers find it and expel him from school. Ramsey is so distressed that he runs to his truck, with Joan following at his heels. They jump in and he drives to a firing range, where he gets out a pistol and begins to shoot at tin cans. When Joan tries to calm him down, he turns the gun on her. Soon the police arrive and cart him off to jail.

God appears in school the next day, in the hallway, to talk to Joan. "I messed it all up," she says. "I'm so sorry. The whole thing was a complete failure."

"It was not a failure. You did exactly what I asked of you," God explained. "All that I asked was that you be present with

Ramsey, and you did that. Do not underestimate the power of your presence. Just being with him is all that I asked of you. Let me show you what would have happened if you had not been present with Ramsey. . . . Do you see that girl by the locker there? She used to make fun of Ramsey. He was planning to shoot her. And that boy over there in the varsity jacket was going to try to intervene. Ramsey was going to kill him too, and then he was going to shoot the vice principal before killing himself. All this was averted, all this evil prevented, simply because you were present with him."

There is no underestimating the power of the laborers who go out into the harvest. They need not go out armed with tactics. They need not have special training. All that God asks of laborers is that they be present with people. Just give the gift of yourself. You may have no idea of the difference that you have made.

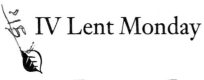

# IV Lent Monday

*"Do you not say, 'Four months more, then comes the harvest'? But I tell you, look around you, and see how the fields are ripe for harvesting. The reaper is already receiving wages and is gathering fruit for eternal life."*

JOHN 4:35–36

## The Abundance of the Harvest

Grain has been humanity's best form of nourishment for thousands of years. The first stalks of wheat were believed to have grown wild in the hills surrounding the Sea of Galilee. Much of the wheat that is grown throughout the world today is genetically similar to the wheat of this region of Israel. This was the mother of all wheat.

In Jesus' time, the harvest was a sign of abundant life. When one walked through fields of wheat, one knew that there would be food for the coming year. And not just bread, but also yeast, gruel, and beer. This was the stuff of life in a time when life was more precarious.

My Russian professor once told me of a Russian woman who, upon visiting a grocery store in America in the 1980s, burst into tears. She had never seen so much food in one place. She was overcome with gratitude, wonder, and awe.

Think of the wheat fields as a full grocery store in the time of Jesus. Think of the magnificence of beautiful, healthy, robust wheat growing as far as the eye can see.

Jesus saw the human need to nourish the body and the joy that people felt at the sight of a field ripe for harvesting. He saw this physical need as secondary to the life of the soul. Would that we could understand that it is eternal life that matters most. Jesus saw human souls as wheat, ripe for the picking. Hundreds and thousands of souls ripe for the picking. They were only in need of guidance to turn their hearts to God.

This metaphor that Jesus uses gives us a glimpse into the joy he must have felt when he told people about God. He did not liken his ministry to grueling, thankless labor. He did not feel that his work was done in vain or had gone unnoticed. Rather, he saw himself as a reaper in the middle of a huge harvest, gathering fruit for eternal life. It was not the labor that was difficult, but only the vast amount of souls in need of harvesting. It was a good problem, to have so much bounty, so much harvest. If he was tired, it was only because the Lord had provided him with such a rich harvest of souls.

God's work was not hard then and it is not hard now. It is joyful work, the best kind of work. It produces a happy kind of exhaustion that comes from abundance of opportunity. Jesus must have been tired, but he also must have been fulfilled.

My favorite part of the week is my Newcomers class. We call it "Basic A," for Basic Anglicanism. I sit with these amazing people. Each of them has been on a journey that led them to this church. Some were Baptists, some Roman Catholics, others have never been to church. They are eager to learn. They ask the most incredible questions, and all I have to do is talk with them, tell them about this amazing tradition of which I am a part, and then sit back and enjoy their experience. I always leave that class renewed, energized, and hopeful. Gathering up the harvest is the best part of my day.

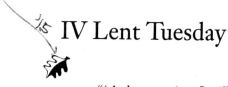

# IV Lent Tuesday

*"'At harvest time I will tell the reapers, Collect the*
*weeds first and bind them in bundles to be burned,*
*but gather the wheat into my barn.'"*

MATTHEW 13:30

## Surrounding Yourself with Wheat

In Kansas, farmers grow the wheat so close together that it becomes difficult for weeds to take root. But some always manage to slip in. So it is with people. Surround yourself with true friends, who neither gossip nor toy with you, and you will find that the weeds in your spiritual life grow fewer. At harvest time there will be less for God to separate. Most of those in your life will continue with you to the heart of God that is heaven.

I married a couple last weekend. They were a beautiful couple, and both came from loving families. Both sets of grandparents had been married for over fifty years. Though the couple chose to be married in a ceremony with modern music and other customs to their liking, the parents and grand-parents did not complain. They understood that the marriage ceremony was to be an expression of the young couple's love for each other.

The groom and I waited in a side room just minutes before the ceremony began. He was nervous, shaky. The groomsmen, both his brothers and his friends, surrounded him. They told jokes to get his mind off the seriousness of this life-changing event. They played poker, slapped him on the back. Just be-fore the ceremony, his best man took him in his arms and told him what an honor it was to support him on this day.

There were no weeds in sight, none of the normal famil-ial dramas that surround most of the weddings I perform. The mother of the bride did not try to control the ceremony. Everyone laughed. It was bountiful.

Once you begin to discipline yourself to live life free of soap-opera drama, once you learn to tell the truth and speak well of others, once you learn to love genuinely and not play games, wheat tends to grow up around you. You will find your-self tiring of those who play games and create drama. You will find that you are inclined to grow wheat all around you, so that there is no longer room for the weeds. And your spiritual wheat will grow stronger with time and practice. And you will thrive for many generations to come.

# IV Lent Wednesday

> *"'Let both of them grow together until the harvest;*
> *and at harvest time I will tell the reapers, Collect the*
> *weeds first and bind them in bundles to be burned,*
> *but gather the wheat into my barn.'"*

MATTHEW 13:30

## Commingling

This parable has many levels of meaning, but here I want to focus on what Jesus is saying about our interior life. We are all made up of wheat and weeds. Just sit down quietly and try to think of God. Weeds will pop up immediately, distracting you from experiencing the love of God. The mind will jump around like a monkey. But in the midst of the weeds, you will also produce wheat of the kingdom. God will find you in strains of silence that make it all worthwhile.

In this metaphor, Jesus reveals one of the essential lessons of prayer. One of the keys to successful prayer and meditation is the ability to let the weeds exist with the wheat. You cannot cleanse your mind as if it were a dirty jacket. There is no way to exorcise those weeds without killing the wheat as well. The key to meditation is to simply notice those weeds and to continue to pray in the midst of them.

Nobel prize winner John Nash struggled with schizophrenia. When first diagnosed, he was treated with shock therapy and medication. But he found that this form of treatment destroyed his genius, clouding his mind. In trying to erase the voices in his head, he also destroyed all creative thought. It was only when he learned to live with these voices, not to silence them, that he was able to continue to work and thrive as a great mathematician.

The mind is a complex creature. There is no way for us to separate the wheat from the weeds. Only God can do that. I would even go so far as to surmise that it is God alone who can determine the difference between wheat and weeds. Some things that we are most proud of might be weeds, and some of our most unproductive thoughts may in fact be holy.

Cultivate time with God, time to nourish your spiritual life. But know that in the midst of the silence, you will find both insight and distraction, clarity and confusion, light and darkness. Let everything grow without censorship, knowing that God alone will free your mind when you meet Christ face-to-face.

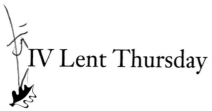

# IV Lent Thursday

*"The harvest is plentiful, but the laborers are few."*

MATTHEW 9:37

## Partnering with God

Wheat is a product of partnership between humans and the earth. It does not grow in abundance naturally. Wheat must be cultivated and nourished by human hands. Though it is hearty, it does not seem to be able to survive without agricultural support. The harvest is the bountiful result of a marriage between God's creation and human hands. In our fallen world, it seems to be the best that we can do.

If God sows spiritual seed, much of that seed is like the wheat: it needs cultivation and human attention. Few souls will find their way to God by themselves. Most of us need one another in order to find God in this fallen world. The gospel harvest is the result of a marriage between God's message and people's love.

I believe that the devout Christian needs three mechanisms

to experience God. The first is private prayer. This is of vital importance, for we all must find ourselves nakedly facing the incomprehensible mystery that is God. The second is corporate worship, the awe-inspiring presence of the Holy as multitudes sing and pray together. The final path to God is what I like to call the House. We need to find God in community, in people, in one another.

I have tried to start small groups in church for years. The scenario is always similar. People claim to have no time, they don't RSVP and often come up with excuses, but once they get involved, it feeds them like nothing else. Granted, some small groups just don't click, but most do. People don't realize how lonely they are until they find the time to sit down together and really talk. This form of devotion assuages loneliness like nothing else. People find God potently in the unconditional love of true community.

When I was fourteen, I went on retreat to a conference center in Massachusetts. Each morning I met in a small group of varying ages. I think there were eight of us. We met for about three hours. On the third day of the retreat, I found myself crying. I had no idea why I was weeping; tears were just pouring down my face and they wouldn't stop. I had no idea why I was in so much pain.

I went to my small-group meeting and the tears just poured

down. I was so embarrassed. I was sure that they would hate me, laugh at me. After all, I had no understanding of why I was so sad. To my surprise, they explained to me why they thought I was in so much pain. Each person took a turn talking with me, and their words cut through my confusion. I was able to see myself in their eyes. I felt loved in a way that I had never experienced before.

At the end of our meeting, they did something that I will never forget. They asked me to lie down on the grass, under a tree where we had been talking on this beautiful summer morning. They all stood around me and lifted me up. They held me there, beneath the tree, and swaying together they rocked me and sang. They loved me as a child and as an adult. And they loved me as I was, right in between.

I was given a glimpse of God's love that morning. To this day, when I feel sad, I envision the hands of the Father, Son, and Holy Spirit holding me. After that day, I felt that I could breathe again. And I needed those people to bring in the harvest for me. I could not have experienced God without their words, their faces, their hands.

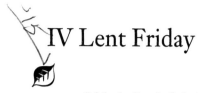

# IV Lent Friday

*"Ask the Lord of the harvest to send out laborers into his harvest."*

MATTHEW 9:38

## Stress and Strength

Craig Minor, the foremost historian of the state of Kansas, notes why wheat became so abundant in the state: "The weather stressed the wheat just enough to bring out its fine milling qualities and give it high protein content." In other words, a harvest of wheat must endure some stress in order to produce a healthy crop. Stress, wind, heat, cold—these are necessary requirements to ensure strength and quality of wheat. That is why Kansans grow winter wheat, because they found that the wheat actually grows stronger if it must endure the stress and hardship of a Kansas winter.

Who would have thought that wheat might benefit from hardship? It is also true in the spiritual lives. Our spiritual lives, like the wheat, become stronger when faced with struggle and hardship. As with the wheat, this hardship cannot be so bad as to kill the wheat. But it must be substantive enough to cause the wheat to be challenged and to grow. The souls within us grow with pain, with suffering and hardship. We were meant to struggle. It is part of the growth process.

My friend Phil lost his wife seven months ago. She was his whole world. They traveled together, collected beautiful pieces of art, lived in three homes, and generally loved life. Phil nursed her until she died, and then he came to a crossroads. He could grieve, retreat into retirement, and disappear, or he could let this incredible loss build his character. He chose the latter. For the first time in his life, he attended a class at the church on the basics of our faith. He began to make more generous donations to charity. He found friendships in the most unlikely places, in people who had no wealth but had warm hearts. I am watching now as he explores his spiritual life properly for the first time. In a way, he is traveling to even deeper realms of existence, and yet none of this growth would have been possible without the pain of his loss. His fiber, his substance was strong enough to withstand the pain and use it to increase the depth of his spiritual growth.

Growth can be painful. Wheat that grows in a land free

of harsh weather does not flourish, but becomes weak and too pliable. It is when the crop is challenged that it rises to abundance. In our suffering we are challenged to find our truest self.

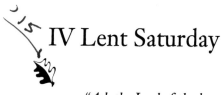

# IV Lent Saturday

*"Ask the Lord of the harvest to send out laborers into his harvest."*

MATTHEW 9:38

## Cutting Back

A Kansas farmer told me about an odd farming practice. After the winter wheat is planted, when it has begun to grow and shoots are reaching up out of the ground, many farmers will put their cattle, horses, even sheep out to graze. "But they eat the young wheat!" I protested. "Yep," he smiled, "but that cutting back that they do, farmers believe that it makes the wheat grow faster and stronger in the end."

I do recall cutting back bushes in my yard so that they would grow in more fully. Most plants are that way too. The process of cutting back brings out flowers, fruits, and more lush vegetation. It is a universal practice.

I am about to meet with a woman to cut back her growth a bit. I believe that she suffers from a kind of depression. This depression has debilitated her family. I have watched her struggle as a member of my parish for three years. I think that it is time to talk to her.

But what will I say? Maybe I'll let her know that I have noticed how she struggles and I'll ask her when she began to feel so anxious, so sad. I will wonder with her if it is possible for her to feel better, and then I will dare to suggest that she might be suffering from depression and hand her a referral to a good psychiatrist.

She will be cut back, no doubt. She might say that this is none of my business or that I am wrong. But she has come to me for counseling before, and I believe that she trusts me. What I tell her will hurt, but if she listens, it could also help.

This kind of news can cut us down for a while. Realizing that we have been struggling with something beyond our control can be paralyzing. But I'm hoping that she may also be relieved.

There is another kind of spiritual cutting back. I have seen it time and time again, when someone becomes overcommitted and must learn to say no. I have seen the most responsible people quit committees and volunteer opportunities because they realize that if they don't cut back, they will be drained. "I feel so guilty," one woman confessed after backing out of a job for which she had volunteered, "but I need more time with my children." And she did need that time. She found her sanity returned when she trimmed down her schedule and had time for herself.

There are many kinds of spiritual pruning. Do not feel that your cutting back is a kind of backtracking. Admitting our frailties, saying no—these are ways that our spiritual lives are given a chance to regroup, to strengthen, to be renewed.

# CHAPTER 6

# Wind

*A Fifth Week in Lent*

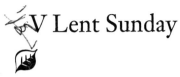# V Lent Sunday

> *"The wind blows where it chooses, and you hear the sound of it, but you do not know where it comes from or where it goes. So it is with everyone who is born of the Spirit."*

JOHN 3:8

## Dancing with God

Living in Kansas has taught me that the wind has moods. At times I want to describe the motion of the air around me, but words prove inadequate. "That's quite a wind!" I'll bellow to my husband as we struggle to pile three small boys into a station wagon. The force of the wind in Kansas can blow you right off your feet. The soft caress of a summer breeze can make you smile. The dance of the wheat at harvest time is a beauty to behold, an unpredictable rejoicing of movement and color. Even light seems to dance in the wind.

Human beings can hear and feel wind, but we cannot see it. We cannot see it because it operates within the very medium

*109*

of our existence. Think of how a fish dwells in the water. The fish can be pushed and pulled in different directions by currents, and yet that fish can neither taste nor tell you about this substance within which it exists. So it is with air. We live in and around it all the time, but only when it moves irregularly do we notice its presence.

The Spirit of God moves in and around us in the same fashion. God exists within and without, and yet we do not notice this third person of the Trinity unless it moves irregularly. We notice it when it becomes impossible to avoid; when it speaks to us in music, art, beauty; when it moves us to tears for no apparent reason. We notice it when we grow unexpectedly into a more mature self or when we find ourselves surprisingly capable of compassion. The Spirit, as the wind, is all around us, always in motion. It is the substance of life itself, but like a fish with water, we can neither describe it nor define it.

In the beginning, God breathed the breath of life into the first human creature. The ancient Hebrew word *ruach* can mean both "breath" and "Spirit." It is both life itself and that which sustains life. It is the very medium of our existence. God is breath itself.

I remember so well the beginning of the movie *Forrest Gump*. The film begins with the simple image of a white feather riding on the wind. The feather dances with ease, sometimes moving quickly, sometimes with slow, swinging movements. One cannot tell which way it will go next. It is completely unpredictable, completely free.

So it is with those who are born again in baptism as Christians. Jesus tries to explain to Nicodemus that those who are born of the Spirit are no longer predictable. Truly living by the Spirit means allowing the unseen to determine the course of your life. It is a frightening prospect, without schedules and without predictions. It means letting go of the control that we as humans crave. It means listening to the movement of the air around you, responding to needs that arise organically as life progresses. It means that you cannot say what tomorrow will bring, only that you will do your best to discern God's Spirit and to follow it. It means that you are about to dance with God, and nothing can be more beautiful or more frightening than that.

Five years ago, one of my parishioners lost his wife. He was the ideal husband right up until her death. He nursed her day and night, refusing to budge from her bedside. He was completely absorbed in her care, and when she finally died, he was more than devastated. He felt unable to live, unable to breathe. He said to me that he felt as if half of his very self were missing. "The better half," he added with a smile. He hid inside his house and could not muster the energy to go to the grocery store.

Fortunately, a rather vivacious and caring woman lived across the street. Daily, she would call and invite him to lunch. He would refuse. "Walter," she would say, "I'm not asking you to marry me! I just want you to go to lunch!" But he could not, he would not.

Finally, one Saturday night at six, she pounded on his door. When he opened to see what was the matter, she spoke forcefully. "Walter, I am taking you out tonight. We are going dancing."

"But I can't dance!" Walter exclaimed.

"It doesn't matter, and I won't take no for an answer," she said, dragging him out of the door and to the car.

Walter found himself at a square dance. He had never been to a square dance in his life. His neighbor dragged him onto the dance floor, despite his continual protests. He found himself stomping around with all these men in cowboy hats. And quite suddenly he realized that he was laughing. He could breathe again. He felt alive. And the most incredible part of it all was that he felt his wife was there with him, that she was laughing with him.

God wants you to live a life of the Spirit. God wants to dance with you.

# V Lent Monday

*". . . you hear the sound of it, but you do not know*
*where it comes from or where it goes."*

JOHN 3:8

## Inspiration

The activity of the wind is a great metaphor for the movement of God. We cannot understand or predict the actions of God. We cannot see God, nor can we be sure that God is present at all. But we can feel God. God can move us to tears. God is as real and as elusive as the wind. And God can change our direction in an instant.

Three days ago my son learned to walk. We were standing in a football field watching his older brother run with the other boys. Max was standing, contemplating his new shoes. He had stood in this way for days, swaying back and forth to keep from falling. But this time something happened. He looked up, saw the other children running on two feet, and something entered his mind. I could see it. His mind expanded in a moment. And he lifted his right foot and took his first step.

Where did that thought come from? Why was he unable to comprehend movement one day and able to do it the next? What other than the Spirit of God, the Logos? It came as a quiet breeze, blowing him into a new level of existence. No wonder we call it *inspiration*.

When the wind blows, we do not know where it comes from or where it is going, but we do know that it changes us in an instant. And we will never be quite the same again.

# V Lent Tuesday

*"And when you see the south wind blowing, you say, 'There will be scorching heat'; and it happens. You hypocrites! You know how to interpret the appearance of earth and sky, but why do you not know how to interpret the present time?"*

LUKE 12:55–56

## The Movement of God

Reading the activity of the earth was a matter of life and death in Jesus' time. This ability to sense a change in climate, the movement of the wind, an expected rain—it was inbred in the smallest child. It was the stuff of survival.

Even today I can feel the rain coming. I can feel the north winds coming down the plain as autumn approaches. I can feel the scorching heat and wonder when the breeze will come again—we all can. If I can sense these things with the insensitivity of an urban being, how much more could the people of Jesus' time anticipate the moods of the earth?

How frustrating it was for Jesus to see the people around him listen so carefully to earth and sky and ignore the movement of God. Even today we tend to think of the spiritual life as elusive, unpredictable, and mysterious, and it is. But it also gives us signals, warnings. Often the Spirit of God gives us a chance to anticipate its movement. But we do not trust our own instincts, and in this way we remain estranged from God, ignoring the signals of the Divine even when they come directly to us.

I know a man who was a child during the bombing of Britain. He now lives the life of a single widower in the United States. For the most part, he is happy and healthy, but he suffers from post-traumatic stress disorder. There are times when he goes out of his mind with unexpected fear, and he has even tried to take his own life.

"Why does God do this to me?" he once asked years ago. "Why not answer my prayers and relieve me of this terrible burden? I am almost self-sufficient, but every once in a while, I find myself in this horrible place. I have to be hospitalized for weeks at a time. And I never know when the blackness will come upon me."

"Do you not know? Are there no signs at all?" I asked.

He proceeded to describe a strong sense of anxiety and obsession, which starts in anticipation of his black periods. He told of his incessant need to ignore these signs and to convince himself that he can master this anxiety.

"But isn't this anxiety the sign that you need?" I asked. "Can you not ask for help at that moment? Why wait until the blackness comes? Why can't you listen to this sign?"

He was at a loss. For decades he had ignored this first warning of his traumatic episodes. What we did was not to eliminate his pain, but to let him see that God was in fact giving him a warning sign.

The Spirit sometimes moves in a way that causes us pain, anxiety, unease. Listen to yourself. If you feel that something is amiss, pay attention. Your discomfort may be the very signal that you need to care for yourself.

# V Lent Wednesday

*Then Jesus cried again with a loud voice and breathed his last.*

MATTHEW 27:50

## Breath

In Jesus' day there was a single word for *breath*, *wind*, and *spirit*. Wind was understood to be the breath of God, blowing across the face of the earth. This same wind was also present in people, as the force of life itself. As God breathed into Adam the breath of life, so each human being has the breath of God. And that breath is life itself.

It is only modern science that has taken us to a place of differentiation between breath, soul, and spirit. For the ancients there was no such distinction. Breath was life, and life was breath. Breath was given to us from God in the same way that God inspires the wind to blow. The wind blows into our bodies, where it resides in life. And one day, in God's time, that same wind will leave our bodies in death.

A few months ago, I stood in a hospital room and watched the body of a sixteen-year-old girl cease to breathe. She had been horsing around on an all-terrain vehicle. There was a terrible accident that left this beautiful blond girl on life support. When the doctors pronounced that she was brain dead, the family had to make a decision. After a lot of tears and sleepless nights, they decided to let her go. Her sister and friends curled her long blond hair and dressed her in her favorite jeans and shirt. They carefully put makeup on her face. When they were ready, we all came into the room.

Turning off life support does not happen all at once. Tubes have to be removed, machines switched off. And then we had to wait as her body struggled to breathe. The nurses had warned us of this, but I had no idea that it could take so long or appear so agonizing. It was as if her young body was simply not willing to let go. Her breathing was labored, raspy; it made her chest heave, and yet it continued. At a loss, I began to talk to her out loud.

"Jennifer," I said. "We are all here with you and we love you. Your body can no longer work right for you. God is waiting to take you home. Don't be afraid. It's okay to let go. We love you so much." The family then began to talk to her as well, giving her permission to go. We sang songs, held her, cried. And slowly her breathing receded until it seemed to slip away into the silence. The whole process lasted about forty minutes.

How can you separate that breath from her soul? It was her life that was leaving us. It was her soul that was struggling to leave the family that she loved. She knew that her death was coming early, and she didn't want to let go. But when she did let go, when the wind left her body, there was peace.

What is the wind? It is the breath of God, the life-giving mystery that inhabits our bodies at once, the rush of air that floods into a child's newborn lungs, the quiet release of the dying breath. How have we come to make a distinction between wind and breath, between soul and spirit? Aren't they one and the same?

# V Lent Thursday

*"God is spirit, and those who worship him must worship in spirit and truth."*

JOHN 4:24

## True Worship

How does one worship in spirit? What did Jesus mean when he uttered those words? Because the word for *wind* and the word for *spirit* were one and the same, what does it mean to worship in wind, in breath, in soul, in life? Does it mean that we no longer have any sort of order to our worship, that we let the wind move us as the Quakers do, waiting for someone to rise and fill the silence with their words?

My best friend in college was Jewish. She and I had long discussions about our faiths, their similarities and differences. She was married just a few years after college, and I was honored to be one of her bridesmaids.

The wedding took place at an inn in the countryside of Massachusetts. The ceremony was beautiful, complete with huppa (a tentlike structure under which the couple exchange vows); they stomped on a glass. But one moment stood out above all the rest. Right after the vows were exchanged, as we were preparing to pray, the rabbi allowed us a moment of silence. And in that silence, the wind blew. It was an enormous gust of wind, blowing instantaneously from out of nowhere, in the middle of a calm day. It was radical, surprising, awe-inspiring. After the ceremony, my friend asked me, "Did you *hear* that wind? What *was* that?"

I smiled. "I only know how to answer that with Christian vocabulary. That was the Holy Spirit." There was no doubt about it: God was present.

I believe in the beauty of ancient liturgy, of words spoken for centuries, molding our consciousness and shaping our souls. But I also believe in following the wind that comes in worship. I believe in engaging in generous silence, allowing time for God to move within us and without. I believe in the wind that speaks to us in music. And I do believe in listening to the congregation and addressing their immediate needs. I have long ago left my notes behind when I preach. I need to look at people, and the Spirit moves me to say things that are beyond my capacity to compose.

Wind. It is unpredictable and a little scary. I find that each worship service is completely and totally unique. Sometimes routine is the way of the day. Some days everyone seems just a little off. And some days the Spirit blows with such passion that I find myself moved to tears. The movement of the Spirit is just like the movement of the wind: ever changing and completely unpredictable.

# V Lent Friday

> *Now some of the scribes were sitting there, question-*
> *ing in their hearts, "Why does this fellow speak in this*
> *way? It is blasphemy! Who can forgive sins but God*
> *alone?" At once Jesus perceived in his spirit that they*
> *were discussing these questions among themselves; and*
> *he said to them, "Why do you raise such questions in*
> *your hearts?"*

MARK 2:6–8

## The Love Letter

I sat across the table from a new member of my congregation. She was young, beautiful. She told me of her professional
life, her relationship with her husband. "Children"—the word
came into my heart like a soft breeze. There was some reason
why she was in pain, and it had to do with children. I pushed
the thought aside. What did I know? I'm not psychic. What if
I was wrong? She would think that I was some kind of quack.

Months later she opened up to me about her fears. She was

unable to become pregnant. . . . So what was that thought that had come to me? Was it the Holy Spirit? Was it some kind of powerful insight? Was it blind luck, a good guess, lucky intuition?

Human beings communicate on many levels. At times the unspoken is louder than words. Intuition is often right. I am slowly gaining confidence in the thoughts that blow through my mind. Often now I will ask, "Is there something more that you want to tell me? I sense that something is left unsaid." Or I will try to openly reflect when someone seems in pain. "You seem to be hurting," I'll say. "Is everything okay?" Often the spirit gives us only a hint of the needs of others, and it is up to us to honestly invite them to fill in the gaps.

The Gospel says that Jesus knew in his spirit that the Pharisees were critical of him. He just knew. Maybe he felt their judgment of his character because of his God-given nature. Or maybe he just knew how to pay attention to the wind of God. Have you ever felt others' criticism without hearing it? Sometimes unspoken aggression is strong enough to blow you off your feet. Hatred can be powerfully felt without a word exchanged. And love can be communicated with nothing but a glance.

At night I often like to sit alone in a small room and watch the trees blowing in the wind. Feeling the presence of God is much like listening to the wind: sometimes it is still, and other times it just rushes in. Because that spirit is unpredictable, we often doubt its presence. But just because the wind isn't blowing doesn't mean that there is no air.

I think that Jesus modeled the kind of intuition that we must all have if we are to follow God. Jesus listened to his intuition; he listened to the spirit of God. He heard unspoken words, needs unexpressed, hearts hungry for God. And this faith in the Spirit of God made his ministry potent enough to carry us for thousands of years.

What if God is writing a love letter to you? What if that love letter lasts the span of your lifetime and beyond? Its words blow through your life in a variety of ways. And it waits to be heard. But in order to listen to that movement, you must be quiet. A gentle breeze cannot be felt if you are running too fast. If you're too active, then you can't tell who is moving, you or the wind. I can best feel the wind when I am stationary and still. Do you dare to hold still and feel the movement of the Spirit? You must be willing to entertain the emptiness of silence, and many people cannot tolerate that. Sit in the emptiness and invite the Spirit wind to blow in and fill the space.

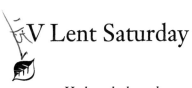

# V Lent Saturday

*He breathed on them and said to them, "Receive the Holy Spirit."*

JOHN 20:22

## Breath

He breathed on them. He blew his wind on them. He gave them his life's breath. What a strange thing to do.

First of all, Jesus was showing them that he was alive. He had breath, soul, spirit, life. He was not a ghost, not an apparition. He was alive. And he was giving them this life.

There is no greater comfort than the breath of someone who loves you. In her book *Uncommon Women*, Madeleine L'Engle tells the story of Emma, a small girl who is not wanted by her mother. After six or seven years of living with her father, she asks to move in with her mother. Though her mother welcomes her, she has set up Emma's bedroom in a carriage house, separate from the mansion in which she lives. Emma's mother parties late into the night, leaving her little daughter alone with a servant. Finally, in tears, she calls for help. Her grandfather tells her that she can come and stay with him for a while.

After a few simple days of living with her grandfather, Emma crawls into his lap and leans against his chest. With the innocence of a child, she is unable to fully express the depth of her pain, but he knows. She leans against him and listens to the gusty wind of his breath, the strong thud of his heart. "Grandfather, my mommy doesn't love me," she admits and begins to cry. "I am anguished by her inability to be a mother to you, child, just anguished," he replies. "Grandfather," Emma asks, "do you love me?"

"You are the child of my heart, the gift that God has given me in my old age," he replies. Leaning against him, hearing his breath, his life, his love, she relaxes. And his love rights her world.

When I am lonely, I sometimes imagine leaning against Jesus like the beloved disciple at the Last Supper. I imagine listening to his breath, the thud of his strong heart. I imagine his love sinking into my soul like the air that I breathe, extending my life, expanding my love and my soul.

No wonder he breathed on them. He loved them after all,

and he wanted them to feel his life and his love. He wanted them to know that, despite all the hatred in the world, despite their despair and loneliness, he was still breathing. And he still loved them.

# CHAPTER 7

# Fig Tree

*A Sixth Week in Lent*

# IV Lent Sunday

*In the morning, when he returned to the city, he was hungry. And seeing a fig tree by the side of the road, he went to it and found nothing at all on it but leaves. Then he said to it, "May no fruit ever come from you again!" And the fig tree withered at once.*

MATTHEW 21:18–19

## Jesus' Power

Sara awoke from her cancer surgery with one thought on her mind: "What did I do to deserve this? I must have sinned terribly for God to allow this to happen to me."

Because the surgeon removed her cancerous organ completely, Sara's prognosis is good. But though it was a clean removal and her odds of survival are very high, Sara nonetheless felt cursed by God.

Hers is a normal human reaction to disease. It is normal to ask: Why me? What have I done wrong? Why would God allow any of my organs to malfunction? Is God cursing me like Jesus cursed the fig tree? We often conclude that our disease is a punishment for somehow having angered God.

Yet this is an Old Testament understanding of God. The ancient Hebrews believed in an angry God, a God who was easily offended, a God who would wipe out entire populations, like the city of Sodom, simply out of anger for their sinfulness. In a time of plague and famine, in an age when people seemed to fall ill and die for no reason at all, pointing to an angry God was the way to explain tragedy. It is a simple theology, easy to believe. And indeed many of us still believe that our misfortunes are a sign of God's displeasure and punishment.

What power Jesus had to sap the life force from a tree without even a moment's hesitation! How frightening to think that he had that ability. And yet, other than in this moment, he does not ever use that ability again. When people come to whip him, to torture and bind him, he does not curse anyone. Why did he remain so passive when he apparently possessed the power to kill them in an instant?

There is no doubt that Jesus willingly sacrificed himself for us. He did not have to hang on that cross. He did that freely for you and for me, and for Sara.

It is God who sustains our every breath, God who gives us the gift of each moment. How can we believe that God has abandoned us when one of our organs malfunctions? Do we forget the others that function just fine, moment by moment, day by day? Instead of giving thanks for the smooth functioning of our bodies, we find ourselves contemplating God in desperation and even anger. "I had not thought about God or the gift of life until I began to die," Betty told me with regret on her deathbed. "I wish that I hadn't waited so long."

Maybe Jesus sacrificed one tree to demonstrate his power, just as he sacrificed himself to show us his love. Or maybe he just lost his temper. This passage reminds us that Jesus had the power to sap life from a living organism, but that he does not do that to us. Even when we condemned him to death, he chose to give us life, his life, eternal life.

# VI Lent Monday

*In the morning, when he returned to the city, he was hungry. And seeing a fig tree by the side of the road, he went to it and found nothing at all on it but leaves. Then he said to it, "May no fruit ever come from you again!" And the fig tree withered at once.*

MATTHEW 21:18–19

## Giving Back

People like to tell me that life is a gift. It's a phrase repeated so often that I think some folks believe it's scriptural. And it sounds so good. For many it comes to mean that God has given us life as a freebie, with no strings attached. But I don't think life is that kind of a gift.

I think God has placed us on this earth for a purpose. Life has been given to us, yes, but not as a free gift. There are expectations involved, a reason for our being. God insists that we give of ourselves. Our lives are not fulfilled until we bear fruit.

This is a new thought for many of us. We live according

to a long-standing myth, a myth that is nearly impossible to shake. The myth is about entitlement. We actually believe that we own the clothes on our back. We believe that we own property, a home, life insurance, even children. Do we really own anything at all? Do any of these things go with us when we die? Can we truly control them? I don't believe that we actually own anything at all. Ownership is a myth, an illusion of this fallen world.

What if our lives are not a free gift, but a chance to serve? What if we have been charged with the responsibility to bear spiritual fruit? What if God expects it of us? What if the only way back home is to produce the fruit, that for which we were created? And what if God can become angry when we do not produce fruit?

During the proper season, the fig tree produces both leaves and fruit at the same time. So when Jesus approached this tree, it was time for it to bear fruit. He was not expecting something that was beyond its capacity. He was merely expecting the tree to fulfill its true nature. The tree was ready, it was time, but there were no figs.

Jesus never judges the fruit itself. All he wants is for the tree to give him something. He wants it to produce *something*. After all, he gave of himself. And we are called to follow his example. "Take," he said. "Eat. This is myself."

Frederick Buechner describes watching killer whales perform at an aquarium. Unexpectedly he started to cry. There they were, twirling and dancing in the air, diving into the clear water, and he was overcome with tears. Why? Because they reminded him of Eden, of that garden where we belong, where we owned nothing at all, where we felt true joy and true freedom.

In Eden we were with God. But for some unknown reason, we took fruit that was not offered to us. And now God asks us to give that fruit back. In fact, I believe that is the only way to come Home. It is our purpose in life, our reason for being. We must give our spiritual fruit to God. No matter how big or how small, no matter how bitter or how sweet, God wants us to give back that which we once took. God wants us to give.

Don't think about how good your gifts may be; don't even consider the quality of your offering at first. Concentrate on the giving, and God will be pleased, because you will be fulfilling the true purpose for which you were created.

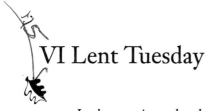

# VI Lent Tuesday

*In the morning, when he returned to the city, he was*
*hungry. And seeing a fig tree by the side of the road,*
*he went to it and found nothing at all on it but leaves.*

MATTHEW 21:18–19

## The Cultivated Tree

In the wild country of Israel, fig trees grow no larger than a
bush. But if they are cultivated and cared for, they can grow as
large as a shade tree, even up to forty feet. If the fig tree in this
passage was growing by the road in the city, it was probably
cultivated; it belonged to someone. It was common for owners
to plant fig trees on the edges of their property, and it was as-
sumed that passersby might pick off a few figs. They were an
excellent, cheap source of nourishment. Due to its location, it
is likely that this fig tree had been nourished, cultivated, well
cared for. Jesus, walking by, would have expected such a tree
to have borne some fruit.

God knows where we come from and what we are capable

of. This was a tree that had grown in the midst of people who would have watered it, cultivating it in the expectation that it would bear fruit for nourishment. So when it does not produce fruit, there is a reason to be disappointed.

Would Jesus have praised the smaller bush that grew in the wild without cultivation but produced fruit nonetheless? I believe that he would have. Blessed are those who are poor and yet produce the fruits of the kingdom.

When hurricane Katrina struck the Gulf Coast, there was a man working on a barge. He phoned his wife, giving her ample warning and instructing her to evacuate their house and find safety. But she did not want to leave him. She stayed at home, sleeping in their bed that night. As the hurricane began to rage, a tree fell on their house and she was killed.

Her husband returned the next day to find his house in ruins. His wife's dead body lay under the rubble. He reportedly carried her body for forty miles, until he found a hospital. I think that he hoped she might have some breath of life still in her. They buried her the next day at a cemetery near the hospital. Bereft, he slept on her grave for three nights.

This was a man who had everything taken from him: his home and the love of his life. Before the tragedy they would sleep with their arms linked together. It was the kind of companionship that is rarely found and often sought. Without her he was lost.

The man arrived at a shelter where one of my parishioners was working with the Red Cross. He was filthy from sleeping on his wife's grave, tired, and hungry. After a bath and some food, he began to visit with the other evacuees, to console them.

"How is it that someone who has nothing can give so much?" my parishioner asked over the phone. "He is blessed indeed," I said. "For he bears fruit even in a barren desert. His wife will be waiting with open arms for him in heaven." I imagine that Jesus must look upon such spiritual fruit and give thanks and praise.

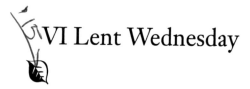

# VI Lent Wednesday

*He went to it and found nothing at all on it but leaves.*

MATTHEW 21:19

## The Search

Yesterday I went out to the tomato plants that my son Jacob and I had planted months ago. Jacob, at age five, has been retrieving most of the ripe tomatoes. He gets excited about waiting until they are just ripe, then picking them and parading them about the house with shouts of "Look at this that God made!"

I found that Jake hadn't been really searching; he had just been looking with the impatience of a five-year-old. When I began to search, I found them: behind branches, covered by leaves . . . ripe tomatoes. They reminded me of nursing, when my breasts would get so full of milk that I just longed for the baby to wake up hungry and drain away my discomfort. These tomatoes were so ripe, they were ready to give themselves up to the ground. They were just waiting for someone to look a little harder.

I can only imagine that Jesus searched that tree for fruit. He must not have left any leaf unturned, any branch unmoved. And as he searched, his frustration must have mounted. Such a tree, with leaves, good soil, bright sun—where was the fruit?

And it makes me marvel that Jesus needed that fruit. As a human being, he was hungry and tired. His body needed nourishment, yet the tree provided none.

Jesus searches all of us in the same manner. He searches for our gifts, our service to him, our nourishment of the kingdom. And it pleases him to no end when he finds a fruit, ripe and ready and still untouched. And oh the joy, the release that we must feel when that ripe fruit is picked, is taken, is eaten. Like nursing, it must be the drought of peace.

If we focus only on Jesus' anger at the tree, we fail to listen closely. Before his anger was his search, his effort, his attention. As the psalmist writes, "Lord, you have searched me out and known me." Jesus searches far and wide for us to be faithful, for us to give. Doesn't that show us just how valuable our fruit is to God? God has created a world in which our response to the Divine love is very important. The kingdom cannot be spread without human hands and voices. God needs our fruit, and God will search high and low for its presence in the world.

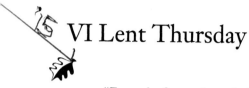

# VI Lent Thursday

*"From the fig tree learn its lesson . . ."*

MATTHEW 24:32

## Chock-Full of Seeds

Writing about the fig tree has made me curious about figs, so I decided to order figs from all over. Turkish figs, local figs, Fig Newtons. They come in all shapes, sizes, even colors. But all figs share one thing in common: they are full of seeds. I have never seen such density of seeds in a fruit. The seeds are packed in; they form the innards of the fruit. There is virtually nothing but seeds and skin.

It is the fruit that we bear that spreads the kingdom of God. Just as the fig tree contains seeds of the kingdom, so our best works, when given to God, spread God's presence. Our gifts are chock-full of God's presence, packed with seeds.

Rosa Parks died recently. Talk about a fruit that was chock-full of seeds! Here was a shy, unassuming black woman who knew that segregation was wrong. She felt that injustice in her bones. But it took her many years to work up the courage to give her gift to her people.

The fruit that Rosa Parks grew became ripe in that moment when she was told to move out of her seat on the bus. She found herself at a critical moment. All that she was, all that she had learned, all the nurture and growth that she had been fortunate enough to have—it all came together in one moment. And in her refusal to move, she bore fruit.

The refusal to give up her seat was Rosa Park's gift to the world. Like the fig, that fruit of dignified resistance was chock-full of seeds of the kingdom. And when she offered herself, the seeds took root and grew. They grew all the way to the Supreme Court.

What if Rosa had not had the courage to refuse to give up her seat? What if she had let her doubts, her insecurities, her confusion cloud her judgment? What if she had listened to the police, the pressure of the media, the voices of hatred? What if she had succumbed to doubt, to reason, to fear? So many seeds would have been lost, so much left unexpressed. She was a champion simply by being herself, ripe and ready at the right moment.

Offering your gifts to God takes courage. Sometimes it takes defiance and sometimes incredible risk. I remember when Jacob, at four, stood up to play "Twinkle, Twinkle, Little

Star" on the violin. There he was up there, so small, so scared. Would he be able to raise the instrument to his chin? Would he say his name? The thoughts flitted across his face; I could see them clearly. Should I run and hide or should I step out and show off? Who am I anyway?

Remember how vital your gifts may be, how full of the potential of God's presence. Do you realize how important it may be for you to dare to present your gifts to others, to let them consume them, taste of your fruit, devour your offering? Do you realize that it has everything to do with the presence of God in the world? You are a vital part of God's creation. You are chock-full of potential. Step out and play your music.

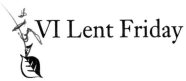

# VI Lent Friday

*"As soon as its branch becomes tender and puts forth its leaves, you know that summer is near."*

MARK 13:28

## Awake Enough to See

When Jesus described the end of days, he told his disciples that they would be able to recognize the time when it came. They would not be able to calculate when; it was not for them to predict. But when Christ came again, it would be made clear to all who were awake.

To make his point clear, Jesus describes the fig tree. Just as you notice when its branch softens and the leaves begin to bud, so you will notice that the earth and sun are changing, telling you that the end is near. Of course, only those who are awake enough to notice the subtleties of nature will be able to see the coming of Christ.

The notion of being awake seems to be central for Jesus. When he looked at that fig tree and noticed the softness that overcomes the wood branches before growth, he was looking closely. He was noticing things that remained outside of his control. He was alive to the movement of nature and the coming of spring.

You have to slow down to notice when a branch softens. You have to touch the branch, hold it, examine it. You wouldn't notice it in just running by. Being awake takes time: time to meditate, time to notice.

In *The Color Purple*, Alice Walker writes, "I think it pisses God off if you see the color purple in a field and don't notice it." God wants us to be awake, to notice the motion of the earth, the moods of our loved ones. Our awareness of God's creation is an integral part of our salvation. We must learn to listen to one another and to God.

A woman at our church loves to paint. She drives out to the middle of the plain, where she sets up her stool, her easel, and her paints, and then she looks. She says that painting has taught her how to be awake. She will look and look until she sees. Something will grab her, speak to her—some beauty, some movement, some light . . . something. And then she knows what to paint. And she will paint and paint, seeing more and more deeply as her painting progresses, until the painting is completed.

If we watch, it seems like the curtain that divides our world from God gets pulled back a bit from time to time. You can catch glimpses of real beauty, true freedom, joy itself. These things await us if we just take the time, like Jesus, to see that the branch grows soft on the fig tree.

# VI Lent Saturday

*"From the fig tree learn its lesson."*

MATTHEW 24:32

## Jesus' Anger

I have often wondered if the fig was the forbidden fruit of the garden of Eden. Scholars can only surmise. It is a possibility, since Adam and Eve dressed themselves in fig leaves once they realized they were naked. If they had eaten the figs off of that tree, they had only to reach for its leaves when they felt exposed.

I suppose we will never know the specific nature of that fruit, or what made Adam and Eve sacrifice their Eden to reach for it. The Babylonian Talmud indicates that the forbidden fruit might have been a fig. The Latin word for sin, *peccare*, is related to the Hebrew word for unripe fig, *pag*. Did the writers of the Gospel have this in mind when they told the story of Jesus' cursing of the fig tree? Was Jesus in some way symbolically reversing the effects of the fall? Or was he simply hungry and irritated?

I think theologians sometimes search for hidden reasons for Jesus' anger. We do this because we find it disturbing that Jesus could get mad, and even more disturbing that Jesus would curse and destroy a tree. Why was he so angry?

I find that I get more angry with my children than with anyone else. Parishioners can insult me, they can be lax or not live up to their promises, and I take this all in stride, but if one of my boys says something rude, I get really mad. There have been times when I have gotten too mad.

Jesus' anger at the fig tree offers us glimpses into his humanity and his love. People get angry only when they care deeply about something. Indifference, however, is much worse than anger. I know a woman who is divorcing her husband after many years not because he is angry or abusive, but because he is simply not present. He never gets mad or sad, and he is never loving. He simply does not care. He is gone from her life, and all she is left with is the shell of a marriage. I think that this woman longs for his anger. She has even tried to provoke him at times, simply to get some kind of reaction. Lack of anger can sometimes be a sign of lack of commitment.

I do think that God gets angry and frustrated with us when

we don't attempt to live fully, when we don't produce spiritual fruit. Nothing angers God more than wasted potential. It is far better to take risks in the spiritual life than to sit back and let the moment pass. God measures our salvation by our investment, our efforts, our love, our action, our commitment. We simply must try. That is all that is asked of us.

# CHAPTER 8

# A Mountain Rising Out of the Sea

*Easter*

# Easter Sunday

*Someone will ask, "With what kind of body do they come?" Fool! What you sow does not come to life unless it dies. And as for what you sow, you do not sow the body that is to be, but a bare seed, perhaps of wheat or of some other grain. But God gives it a body as he has chosen, and to each kind of seed its own body.*

1 CORINTHIANS 15:35–38

It happened in Children's Chapel about three weeks ago. There was a bit of a fiasco that Sunday morning. A new little girl came and boldly went upstairs with the kids. She unknowingly sat in the seat of one of our faithful, strong-willed boys. This little boy thought it best to simply lift her off her feet and transplant her to another spot in the circle. He was about to do just that when one of our deacons intervened. "We must let our guest stay in the seat that she chose," explained the deacon. After all, the little girl was a guest.

At the prospect of having to sit in another seat, this little boy had what I call a meltdown. It happens when the body of a little boy melts into something unable to stand. Tears come, and yelling too. In the middle of this scene, another four-year-old stood up and put his hand on his hips as if he were about to deliver an important lecture. "Tommy," he said, "You are having *an issue*. Everyone has issues. It's time for you to make a *better choice*. This is an *issue*."

Deacon Patsy would later report that she watched as one boy melted and the other parroted his mommy's lectures. And she thought to herself, "My goodness, they are acting just like the adults in church."

It doesn't take much for human beings to become distracted from God. We spend much of our time in church and outside church consumed with details. Does someone have my seat? What is my place in life? Am I successful? Where will I spend my next dollar?

You and I could spend our whole lives living in just this way, living normally, and never have one original thought, because we are not fully awake.

There was a man who worked in Switzerland in the early twentieth century as a technical examiner third class. By all standards his life was nothing special. He had a child out of wedlock, he failed to pass his entrance exams to the university and had to take them again. He was not affiliated with a university. He did not even have access to a very good library when he wrote a few articles for an obscure physics journal. That man was Albert Einstein.

Albert Einstein was able to free his mind. We are not certain how or why, but by the grace of God, he did not let his failures in life define who he was. His first few articles would change the way that we see the world, and yet, even after they were published he was denied a job as a high school teacher and had to go back to work as a technical examiner third class. Einstein freed his mind to imagine a universe full of possibility. He had an original idea. For whatever reason, this man was able to wake up and see something new.

When the disciples ran to the tomb, Peter and James were shocked to see that the body of Jesus was missing. They immediately ran away to tell the others, to process this disturbing news, to give a report of what they had seen. Mary Magdalene stayed behind, and for whatever reason, she was able to free her mind. When she looked into the tomb, she did not see just the absence of a body, she saw two angels sitting there. And even after seeing them, she did not leave, but stayed at the tomb, crying. When Jesus came to her, even when he stood before her, she could not open her mind enough to recognize him. She thought that he was the gardener. When Jesus spoke her name, her mind cleared, and in an instant she recognized her love, her master, her life.

There is no way to glimpse the Resurrection without freeing your mind. The event that occurred that Sunday morning is inconceivable. It is the reason Christianity exists. You see, no one had really paid attention to this obscure teacher from Galilee—not until he rose from the dead. The earliest Christian writings were not the Gospels, they were the Epistles, the letters that were sent from people who had come to believe in the Resurrection event and now wanted to know who this man was. The Gospels were written down in an attempt to recall what Jesus did in his life only after people realized that he must have been the Son of God.

A recent article on the cover of *Newsweek* describes how the claim that one man had literally returned from the dead—the event of the Resurrection—had never been made in the history of the world. Sure, other religions had conceived of immortality, but not that a mortal, a human being could actually die and then return. This was inconceivable, and still is.

The Resurrection cannot be understood, but it can be glimpsed. We can catch glimpses of it when we free our minds. Recent events like the controversy over Terri Schiavo, the woman in a persistent vegetative state who ultimately died after the removal of her feeding tube, remind us of how we can get caught up in the details of the moment and forget the big picture. It's as if we have forgotten that there is more to the universe than death. If we really believe that our existence continues after death, then Schiavo's life did not end, it merely moved into the next phase of existence. In the context of the Resurrection, she is more alive now than ever before.

Free your mind. Picture a mountain rising up out of the sea. What you can see from the water level and up is magnificent, high and mighty. But there is so much more that is vast and big and rich found under the waters. You and I can admire so much about this life, but there is so much more to our existence that we simply can't see yet.

Eternal life is not something that begins when we die. Eternal life was given to you when you were baptized, the moment that you pledged to live in God's love. Eternal life abides in you now. At this very moment, you exist in a dimension far beyond human perception. Angels dance in front of your eyes, waiting for you to see them. God's love for you is boundless, exists beyond time and forever. Like the mountain above the sea, you see only a fraction of your true self. Never let others define who you are. For all eternity you will be waking up to this fact—to the self that you are in God.

I believe that resurrection is not something that can be understood or captured. We can only begin to glimpse this miracle when we realize how little we know. Do we really understand how a seed becomes a plant? Do we know how this happens, why it happens? What makes the seed begin to grow? We really know very little about the inner workings of even the simplest events in the creation. If the seed itself is a miracle beyond our understanding, how much more so is resurrection?

Free your mind. Don't squabble about your place in this small society that we live in. God has made you more than you can ever imagine. Our brains understand so little. Trust that there is more than what you can see or understand. Dive into the waters. Witness the mountain of mystery that is God's love, and shout your praises. For it is unbelievable. He is risen! And with him, we all are made whole.

Amen.

# Conclusion

I hope that these Lenten meditations have given you a new sense of awe for the depth of Jesus' words. The simple images that Jesus used from nature are so profound, they are like Zen koans, like great works of poetry whose meaning cannot be encapsulated. They are endless. As you awaken to the beauty of the world around you, I pray that you may see many more dimensions to Jesus' parables of planting. This book just scratches the surface of the meaning. There is much more.

The Incarnation of God teaches us that God is willing to communicate with us in our own language, by becoming human. God wants to tell us stories, paint us pictures, touch us and heal us. The stories and images that Jesus uses in the Gospels have not only a durability but an incomprehensible way of meeting you where you are. Their meaning grows as your spiritual understanding grows. They are stories with meaning that has no end.

I have come to believe that the greatest wisdom is often present in simplicity, in a sparscity of words, a brief moment of insight. No doubt the disciples and others hardly heard all of Jesus' words. It pains me to think of all the images and all the stories that were lost simply because the people around Jesus were distracted, driven by their own needs and desires, and not open to listening.

The act of listening is hard. Listening to Christ is much harder still. To this day he speaks to you through these parables. But you can hear the depth of his message only by stopping your activity and giving your time and undivided attention to God, if even for a few minutes.

The spiritual life is an organic process. Remember to be gentle but consistent, disciplined but free to express yourself. God is within you and outside you. You need only awaken and listen to find God's peace.

Jesus faced tempter bef set out on own ministry — transferance

We were designed for Eden — innocence & joy

Xn hope

What does it look like when the openness is repaired?

Joy different from pleasure